OTHER BOOKS BY JIM GRANT

A Common Sense Guide
to Multiage Practices
(with Bob Johnson)

Developmental Education in the 1990's

Every Parent's Owner's Manuals
(Three-, Four-, Five-, Six-, Seven-Year-Old)
(with Margot Azen)

"I Hate School!" Some Common Sense
Answers for Parents Who Wonder Why,
Including the Signs and Signals
of the Overplaced Child

Jim Grant's Book of Parent Pages

Worth Repeating: Giving Children
a Second Chance at School Success

Childhood Should Be A ~~Pressure~~ Precious Time
(Poem Anthology)

VIDEOS BY JIM GRANT

Accommodating Developmentally Different
Children in the Multiage Classroom

The Multiage Continuous Progress Classroom

Do You Know Where Your Child Is?
What Every Parent Should Know
About School Success

Worth Repeating

Our special gift to help you,
The ultimate change agent

Feel free to reproduce any of the pages of this book,
for educational purposes, within your school.

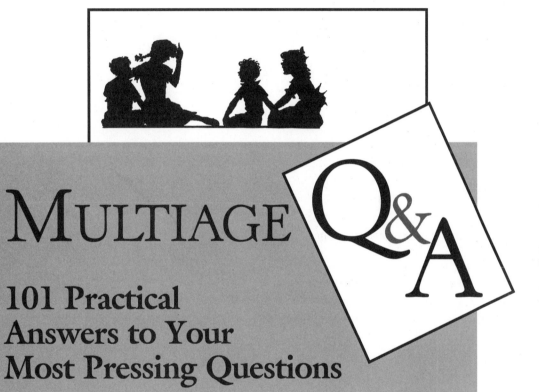

MULTIAGE Q&A

101 Practical Answers to Your Most Pressing Questions

Written and Compiled by
Jim Grant
Bob Johnson
Irv Richardson

Printed in the United States of America

Published by Crystal Springs Books
Ten Sharon Road
PO Box 500
Peterborough, New Hampshire 03458
1-800-321-0401

Publisher Cataloging-in-Publication Data

Grant, Jim, 1942-
      Multiage q & a : 101 practical answers to your most pressing questions /
written and compiled by Jim Grant, Bob Johnson, Irv Richardson.--2nd ed. / rev.
[160] p. : cm.
Includes bibliography, resources and index.
Summary: A compilation of the questions most often asked of the authors as
they lecture on multiage issues. Answers cover multiage philosophy, implementation,
pitfalls, inclusion and other issues.
ISBN 1-884548-08-3
1. Teaching. 2. Learning. 3. Nongraded schools. 4. Team learning
approach in education. I. Johnson, Bob, 1942- . II. Richardson, Irv, 1956- .
III. Title.
371.302 ' 82--dc20   1996   CIP
LC Card Number : available from publisher

Senior Editor: Aldene Fredenburg
Editorial Consultant: Deborah Sumner
Book and cover design: Susan Dunholter
Project Assistant: Marguerite Bellringer
Type Compositors: Christine Landry
                  Laura Taylor

To my wife Lillian, for her belief in my quest to change the plight of overplaced children; without her unfailing support, this book would never be. And to my sons, Nathan and Caleb, for their understanding of my mission and their willingness to share me.

— Jim Grant

To my wife Phyllis, whose vision was greater than mine. Her support and encouragement has enabled me to pursue a lifelong ambition—advocating for children by supporting their teachers.

— Bob Johnson

To my wife Katie, for always, always supporting me when a new challenge arose. And to my two wonderful children, Jamie and Amanda, for being patient with me when I wasn't at home and for letting me experience the joys of parenting when I was.

— Irv Richardson

Contents

Acknowledgments

The authors would like to thank the following multiage educators who contributed their time and expertise in answering one or more questions in this book:

Ed Albert, Ph.D.
Robbe E. Brook, M.Ed.
Gretchen Goodman, M.Eq.
Donna V. Hale, M.S.
Bernie Hanlon, MS.Ed.
Jean R. Hill, Ph.D.
Phoebe Ingraham, M.Ed.
Abby Klein, Ed.M.
Elizabeth J. Lolli, Ph.D.
Diana Mazzuchi, M.Ed.
Beth Ogden, M.E.
Mary Garamella Paulman, M.A.
Elizabeth Quinn

Charles Rathbone, Ph.D.
Joe Rice, M.A.Ed.
Robert J. Ross, M.Ed.
Kathryn Sproul, M.E.
Ellen Thompson, M.Ed.
Jan Ulrey
Dave Ulrey, M.Ed.
James Uphoff, Ph.D.
Marsha Winship, M.S.
Esther Wright, M.A.
Louise Wrobleski, M.E.
Yvette Zgonc, M.Ed.

We also thank Charlotte Keuscher, Program Consultant for the California Department of Education, for contributing information on the California Alliance for Elementary Education and the Multiage Learning Task Force.

Irv Richardson also thanks the following people for their help and support over the years: Bob Lyman; Robert Cartmill; the wonderful staff at Mast Landing School; the parents and students of the Freeport Public Schools, with whom he had the privilege to work.

The authors add a special note of thanks to Senior Editor Aldene Fredenburg, who contributed her time and editorial savvy to help make this project come alive; to Editorial Consultant Deborah Sumner, who lent her editorial and educational expertise; and to Project Assistant Marguerite Bellringer, who collected and organized the original data from all our contributors.

Preface

Working on this book has been like a trip through my childhood. I grew up in a traditional, graded school system, and remember the academic and social categories that some of my classmates ended up in, and, throughout their twelve years of schooling, couldn't seem to escape.

There was Billy, who was restless, had the worst handwriting in the class, and had bad grades. Our second-grade teacher made the kids who misbehaved stand in the wastebasket; Billy was in the wastebasket a lot.

Billy also won two dollars in an art contest in second grade. The local utility company asked our class to design safety posters; the teacher passed out construction paper, and we got to work. Billy requested a piece of black construction paper. "You don't want black construction paper," the teacher said. Billy insisted. He cut letters and a silhouette of a person out of white paper, and arranged them on the black. The letters said, "Wear White at Night." The whole class was in awe.

Sometime during sixth grade we all took an IQ test, and were divided up into the A and B groups going into seventh grade. Billy ended up in the B group. So did Ruthie, a sweet, bubbly girl who never had a bad word to say about anybody, and Winnie Guy, who wrote beautiful poetry. Both Ruthie and Winnie Guy had had among the highest marks in the class, day after day, in the sixth grade. Billy and Ruthie made it through high school; Winnie Guy quit in the eleventh grade.

That every child comes into this world with talents and abilities, and with so much potential to contribute to this world, is the foundation of multiage education and developmentally appropriate practices.

Most of the people who contributed to this book are educators who practice multiage education in their schools. In addition, many of them lecture on multiage practices and developmental education at conferences and seminars around the country. These energetic people have made it their goal to find the treasures hidden in each child, and to help others do the same.

Irv Richardson, for many years an elementary school teacher, got into education to "change the world," and became attracted to multi-age education in particular, because, as he says, "The more I got to know kids the more I realized that they just didn't fit into the little boxes that we tried to put them in."

That the many people involved in creating this book have had the opportunity to so positively impact their students' lives is largely due to the efforts of the founder of The Society for Developmental Education, Jim Grant, and his senior associate and good friend Bob Johnson, who has been with SDE since its inception. Their mission for over two decades has been to give educators the knowledge to help all children succeed in school and in life. Children like Billy.

I wish multiage education had been around for Billy, and Ruthie, and Winnie Guy. I'm glad it's around for their kids.

> — *Aldene Fredenburg*
> *Editor*

What is Multiage Education?

Q.

What are the basic elements of a multiage primary?

A. Like any good educational program for children, there are many components necessary in order to provide a quality multiage primary program.

When a young child enters a multiage program, the curriculum should be appropriate for her level of development. Put a different way, it is the responsibility of educators to ensure that schools are ready for children instead of making children ready for school. The curriculum should be taught through experiences that help children construct knowledge about subject matter. Often the curriculum is taught through a thematic or integrated manner.

The adult working with the students should possess personal qualities that make the environment a nurturing one for children. The teacher should structure the environment so that young people feel safe and free to learn. The teacher needs to be trained in early childhood practices and in early childhood models of instruction.

Parental and community involvement is an important component to education. This is particularly true for a multiage program, since the organization of the program is usually different than the one most parents experienced in their own schooling. Parents should have a voice in the organization of the program as well as having opportunities to volunteer in the school.

Members of the community who do not have children enrolled in the school should also be involved through awareness sessions and with opportunities to do volunteer work with students.

A quality multiage program should have procedures and instruments in place to monitor student progress and to judge its overall effectiveness. The evaluation procedures should be congruent with the ways in which students are taught. Ideally, assessment should be built into the teaching and learning that occur daily in the classroom, rather than relying on standardized testing that occurs once a year.

The program itself also needs to be continually monitored. The information gained from assessment is used to improve a student's instructional program and the overall effectiveness of the multiage program.

A. Multiyear placement simply means that the students stay with the same teacher for more than one year. The multiage and the looping classrooms are the best examples of a multiple-year classroom.

In the looping configuration, a single-grade class stays together like a family and is promoted with the teacher for two and sometimes three years. In the multiage configuration, there are multiple blended grades and the students stay with the same teacher(s) for two or three years.

Many of the benefits of being in a multiage classroom also accrue to students that are placed in a single-grade, consistent setting with a significant adult for more than one year. Benefits realized in a multiple-year setting include:

- Fewer student/teacher transitions.
- A cohesive family atmosphere.
- A higher level of discipline.
- Improved student attendance.
- An increased sense of stability for students as a result of classroom routine and consistency.
- One group of students for the teacher to get to know every other year.
- One group of new parents for the teacher to get to know every other year.
- An increase in mental health benefits for the students.
- A tendency for a decrease in special needs referrals.
- More time-efficient instruction.
- Fewer grade-level retentions.
- Postponement of teachers' high stakes decisions about retention and special education referrals.
- An increased cooperative spirit between students and teacher.
- An increase in parental involvement.
- Semi-seamless curriculum.
- Increased student observation time for the teacher.

Q.

What is meant by multiyear placement?

Educators should be alert to several potential pitfalls of keeping students with the same teacher more than a year:

- There is always the chance, however slight, that a child will be placed with a poor teacher too long.
- A personality conflict between the teacher and the student may prove uncomfortable for both.
- A teacher may inadvertently overlook a child with a learning disability when grade barriers are deemphasized.

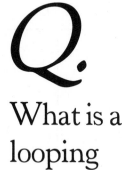

Q.

What is a looping classroom?

A. It is a multiyear placement for both the students and the teacher. A teacher, for example, would begin with a second-grade class, and continue with the same class through the third grade. He would then begin again with another second-grade class. This arrangement requires the collaboration of two teachers as well as the permission of the students' parents.

There are many reasons for the popularity of looping. It is a low-risk concept that requires little funding and minimal training, and only a short lead time for implementation. It doesn't require additional classroom space, and is not considered as an experimental or pilot program.

Numerous benefits accrue when a teacher stays with his students for more than one year:

- Students have only half the teacher transitions.
- The teacher has fewer parents with whom to relate over a longer period of time.
- Attendance improves.
- Overall, the discipline improves.
- The curriculum becomes semi-seamless.
- Learning time increases.

Many educators prefer looping as a preliminary step to fully implementing a multiage classroom.

The most complete information on looping can be found in the book, *A Common Sense Guide to Multiage Practices*, by Jim Grant and Bob Johnson.

A. Perhaps the most concise definition of continuous progress practices can be found in the book entitled *How to Change to a Nongraded School*, written by Madeline Hunter and published by the Association for Supervision and Curriculum Development (ASCD). In the book, Hunter explains that

> "continuous progress refers to a student's progress from time of school entry until graduation. With continuous progress, students are challenged appropriately according to their ability to master intellectual, physical, emotional, and social tasks at progressively more difficult levels. Continuous progress mandates that students should neither spend time on what they have already adequately achieved, nor proceed to more difficult tasks if they have not yet learned materials or acquired skills essential to that new level of knowledge."

Q.

What is meant by continuous progress practices?

Q.

What does a continuous progress curriculum look like?

A. The premise of the continuous progress curriculum is that every child is unique and has an individual pattern and timing for growth. It provides opportunities for children to build progressively on their developing knowledge base. There is respect for different learning styles and paces. It is understood that the time it takes for children to reach certain developmental levels is a variable, prompting the elimination of grade-level barriers or time-based finish lines. Teachers structure a supportive learning environment where children feel successful and competent, develop positive self-concepts, and are helpful and sensitive to others.

Specifically, the continuous progress curriculum has the following characteristics:

• It is integrated. Separate subjects are replaced by an integrated curriculum which engages children in meaningful activities that explore concepts and topics relevant and meaningful to children's lives.

• Whole language, a developmental approach to teaching reading and writing, is the basis of the language arts program.

• Continuous progress accepts each child at his or her place on developmental learning continuums. These continuums contain benchmarks which clearly define major stages of growth. They allow teachers to assess, evaluate, and plan curriculum.

• It reflects an understanding that children construct knowledge and learn through active involvement and play.

• It is embedded in a learning environment where children cooperate and everyone is a teacher/learner.

• Open-ended activities provide for a wide range of abilities, allowing each child to work at his or her developmental ability level.

• Ongoing assessment and evaluation of each child's learning replaces practices such as tracking, retention, and promotion.

• It emphasizes the development of the whole child in the intellectual, social, emotional, artistic, aesthetic, and physical realms.

• It provides for both teacher-directed and child-initiated activities.

A. No. In a multiage continuous progress class, the students have the same teacher for more than one year. This allows the teacher to better know her students and to be able to use this information over a two or three year period of time as she works with the students.

Creating a multiage continuous progress classroom is usually done for philosophical and educational reasons. Educators who start such programs often initiate them because they believe that the graded structure doesn't always meet children's needs and that students benefit from having the same teacher for more than one year.

A combination/split-grade class often exists only for a one-year period. It is usually created for budgetary reasons or because there are too few students to justify two different classrooms. Staff in a combination or split grade report great difficulty teaching and managing two separate grade levels.

The difficulties in implementing combination grade classrooms are described in *Teaching Combined Grade Classes: Real Problems and Promising Practices*, a joint study by the Virginia Education Association and the Appalachia Educational Laboratory:

> The consensus on difficulties [experienced in combination grade classrooms] by 83 percent of the respondents can be capsulized in the response "double planning, double teaching, double grading, and double record keeping." These teachers cited specific difficulties indicating, as one teacher stated, "The time factor is most critical — time in terms of covering materials with students." The individual difficulties reported by teachers that relate to the "time factor" in daily class instruction in order of frequency are as follows:

Q.

Isn't a split or combination grade the same as a multiage continuous progress classroom?

- lack of class time for instruction of two grade levels (71%);
- insufficient planning time (62%);
- not enough time for teachers to master two curricula in preparation to teach (48%);
- insufficient time to effectively cover two sets of curricula (45%);
- never caught up on written work (38%);
- insufficient time to remediate or work on a one-to-one basis with a child (24%); and
- inability to go beyond basics (e.g., not enough time for science experiments) (7%).

A. Yes! One of the major benefits of cooperative learning is the development of social skills. In a multiage classroom children not only learn academically, but benefit from one another socially. Leadership, communication, and conflict management skills can be learned through the use of cooperative learning; this contributes to the success of the multiage classroom. Younger students have a tendency to look up to older students; as a result, when two students of different ages work together, the younger student's interest level, and therefore the amount of subject matter retained, will be enhanced.

The older student, meanwhile, will have an incentive to organize his thoughts, and will be able to take pride in his and his younger partner's accomplishments. Collaborative skills will be heightened and friendships strengthened.

Teaching students interpersonal and small-group skills produces both short-term and long-term outcomes (Johnson and Johnson 1989). Short-term outcomes include greater learning, subject retention, and critical thinking. Long-term outcomes include greater employability and career success.

An individual's quality of life as an adult depends largely on his social skills. Socially skilled people tend to be psychologically healthy. For these and many other reasons, we need to teach students skills necessary to build and maintain cooperative relationships with others. (Johnson and Johnson 1989).

Q.

Is cooperative learning critical to the success of a multiage classroom?

Q.

Are learning centers and work stations vital to a multiage classroom?

A. Yes! Learning centers are vital to any classroom structure that intends to individualize education and allow students to have some control over their own learning. In a multiage setting, the maturity level is great (greater than the chronological age span), so the need for independent learning opportunities is critical.

Combining children into mixed-age classrooms without adjusting teaching and assessment practices is asking for failure. A mixed-age setting demands individualized and small-group teaching strategies. Setting goals, providing instruction, and assessing growth and development all must be done on an individual basis. This is one of the strengths of a multiage classroom.

The materials found in learning centers and work stations should not simply be the same worksheets and workbooks used in a traditional classroom. Designing a program around learning centers takes more than simply changing the furniture. Learning centers need to be designed to nurture children's inquisitive natures and promote experiential learning opportunities and cooperative group activities. Learning centers should actively engage children in the process of learning through the use of manipulatives, creative projects, and open-ended activities. Integrating the curriculum through thematic planning is the first step in creating interesting learning centers that will entice children to learn.

Providing a range of developmentally appropriate activities that meets the needs of children of various ages can be done very effectively in a center-oriented situation. Materials and tasks can be available at a variety of levels, so that each child experiences the challenge of difficult work while being able to enjoy easier tasks.

Learning centers allow teachers an opportunity to observe children engaged in their work and to arrange for small-group and individual conferences. Learning centers also facilitate ongoing assessment that allows for immediate reteaching as necessary.

Student ownership in the learning process is an important benefit of learning centers. Children in such settings are first taught how to learn, rather than what to learn. The classroom that effectively uses learning stations will be filled with choices that allow children to take responsibility for their learning. The teacher is involved in the planning and completion of each child's activities, yet the child is allowed to take as much ownership in the process as she is capable of managing. Children should, at times, be practicing learning processes independently, collaborating with other children and verifying their progress with the teacher during conferences and informal interactions.

Multiage classrooms that are heterogeneously grouped to foster cooperation and individualization must contain a multitude of activities to interest, teach, and challenge every child. One of the best ways to achieve this is through the use of effective learning centers.

Q.

Is it possible to have a multiage program within a graded school?

A. Yes, but teachers of such programs need to spend time and energy educating members of the school community about multiage education, and must be able to address the concerns of these school members, who hold a variety of perspectives. Students, parents, staff members, and administrators all have points of view that need consideration.

Members of the educational community need to understand what the multiage program is and what it is not. Students may think it's for all the "slow" kids or all the "smart" kids. Students placed in the multiage program need to know that academic goals set for them are the same as those in the graded classrooms.

Multiage students should not be isolated from their graded counterparts. Multiage teachers need to ensure that their students eat lunch, have recess, and are given other opportunities to interact with students from other classes on a regular basis.

Parents probably require the most education about this different kind of classroom, since their attitudes and beliefs will influence those of their children. Many think such programs are unstructured, that older or more advanced students spend their days tutoring others, and that children are not receiving the same instruction as students in the graded program.

All of these issues can be addressed by inviting parents in during the school day and/or providing informational meetings in the evenings. Sending home classroom newsletters and sharing current articles about multiage instruction are also beneficial. Putting parents of new students in touch with parents of "veterans" may be the most powerful means for alleviating their fears of the unknown.

Staff members can be the most difficult of audiences. Teachers of multiage programs need to share their beliefs and methods in nonthreatening ways with staff. Without the support of their colleagues, multiage teams may face failure. Negative attitudes and criticism are bound to leak out to community members. Visitations and peer-coaching situations should be encouraged so that staff members and parents can observe a multiage classroom in action.

Multiage teams should not set themselves apart. Having lunch and sharing resources with other teachers, and respecting others' beliefs and methods, are small but significant ways to foster positive peer relations.

Administrators have a most critical role: to foster an understanding of, and tolerance for, a "school within a school" without dividing the staff. Bad attitudes, resentment, and false judgments may occur without strong leadership. School leaders must also ensure that multiage classrooms do not become "dump and hope" programs. Balance is a very important component in any classroom and multiage programs should reflect the whole school's population (Grant and Johnson 1994). Also, scheduling, planning time, and physical space issues will need special consideration.

Q.

What is
outcome-based
education?
Is it compatible
with multiage
continuous
progress
practices?

A. Many of the concepts behind outcome-based education have always been a part of the educational process, although the term "outcome-based" came into educational circles in the 1980s. Any teacher who has ever stated an objective to the class has a desired outcome for her students. Having first graders learn to read is an academic expectation of both the parents and the classroom teacher. Although outcome-based education has been misunderstood and criticized, having educational goals is actually something that all educators, parents, students, and the general public want.

Along with outcomes, there must be transitions or benchmarks along the way, so that a teacher can measure her success at achieving the desired outcome. For example, for K-3 students in a multiage continuous progress class, the outcome may be:

> After participating in the Multiage Program for four years, all students will correctly punctuate simple sentences.

One advantage of both goal-based education and the multiage classroom is that students are not forced to learn content within a rigid framework of 180 days. Students learn material when they are developmentally ready, thus achieving the outcome at their own pace.

A. Multiage education is an organizational structure in which students are placed in a classroom on criteria other than the number of years they have spent in school. A multiage organization may not eliminate all inappropriate practices. However, as a way to organize a classroom, it allows more developmentally appropriate education to occur.

Multiage classrooms are most successful when they are started with a philosophical belief about the type of experiences appropriate for young children. These programs often have a continuous progress curriculum that allows children to make academic progress at their own rates. This type of curriculum is more appropriate for young children than a curriculum that places rigid grade-level expectations on children and forces children to do things for which they are not ready.

Children in multiage classrooms are placed with a classroom teacher for more than one year. This multiyear placement allows the student to bond with the adult for a longer period of time than the conventional single-grade placement.

Q.

Does the multiage nongraded classroom eliminate developmentally inappropriate practices?

A teacher has to spend the first few months of the school year getting to know a new student and her academic, social and emotional needs. With continuous multiage placement, a teacher can build on the previous year's experience with the child, and not have to start over.

In a multiage situation, children get to experience a variety of roles. In a three-year program, for instance, students experience being a younger child in the program, being in the middle, and then becoming one of the older students in the classroom.

In any organizational structure, it is what happens within the structure that makes a difference for children. While a multiage structure may not totally eliminate every developmentally inappropriate practice, it does facilitate the occurrence of many developmentally appropriate instructional practices.

Q.

What exactly are the differences between multiage instructional practices and developmentally appropriate practices used in a single-grade classroom?

A. None. The needs of individual children still must be met through a quality program of instruction, regardless of the span of abilities and age ranges of their classmates.

Both multiage and developmentally appropriate single-grade classrooms should have a literacy program that helps children develop a love for reading through exposure to quality literature, while improving their ability to decode and comprehend text. A math program appropriate for young children would incorporate the National Council of Teachers of Mathematics (NCTM) standards and would focus on using manipulatives and a variety of other activities to help children build a sound foundation of mathematical concepts. Programs for science should involve children exploring their world while using appropriate scientific materials and processes. Curricula for other subjects should also be taught in ways that are congruent with how young children learn.

For information about what activities are developmentally appropriate for children at different ages, read *Developmentally Appropriate Practice in Early Childhood Programs Serving Children From Birth Through Age 8* (Sue Bredekamp, ed.) and other books published by the National Association for the Education of Young Children (NAEYC). Other good books on developmentally appropriate practices include *Yardsticks*, by Chip Wood, and *A Notebook for Teachers: Making Changes in the Elementary Curriculum*, both of which are published by the Northeast Foundation for Children; and *Developmental Education in the 1990's* by Jim Grant, published by Modern Learning Press.

A. No. The need for two-year kindergartens and transitional first grades may be reduced when a district has an effective multiage program in place. It is not eliminated, especially in larger-enrollment districts.

It is vital that multiage programs be widely available and commonly used. This assumes much more than just a grouping of different ages together. It requires methods, materials, time schedules, and curriculum which support such a program. Multiage is not just multigrade!

When integrated curriculum, hands-on and activity-based learning, strong literature-based instruction, and cooperative learning are integral to the program, then the multiage program is likely to be an effective one. When pupils experience an effective multiage program, fewer of them may need an extra year of learning time within their primary program.

If either the availability or quality of multiage programs is restricted, the need for readiness kindergartens and transitional first grades will continue to exist. These programs have been very productive and positive for children, and can continue to meet a real need for some pupils (Uphoff 1995).

Multiage programs are a major step toward providing children with the quality of instruction that, too often, only the extra-year programs provided previously.

Q.

Does a multiage classroom eliminate the need for a transitional kindergarten for young fives or a transitional first for young sixes?

Q.

Is a pre-first/first multiage blend a viable alternative to a self-contained pre-first program?

A. Yes! The birth of the pre-first concept in 1966 in New Hampshire was a valiant attempt to break the stranglehold on the inflexible lockstep graded structure. This additional grade level was designed to build in a year of extra learning time for those children who are chronologically six but are developmentally too young and simply need three years to complete the traditional kindergarten and first year program. Thousands of extra-year programs were created as an alternative to school failure. These programs enjoyed great popularity with parents and teachers for the most part; they did what they were intended to do. These programs incorporated developmentally appropriate practices, reduced teacher, parent, and child stress, promoted a child's self-esteem, negated retention, and enhanced performance for many students.

Most school systems that have eliminated the extra year of learning time did so not because it didn't work, but because of the cost of financing the extra year. The program was replaced with the age-old concept called social promotion.

Social promotion is the practice of moving students up through the grades without giving consideration to the students' developmental needs or skills attainment. Social promotion creates a host of other school ills, such as an increase in school-induced learning disabilities and attention deficit disorder, low academic performance, and an increase in discipline problems. Some classroom educators reacted to the loss of this extra learning time option by creating a very real substitute — a pre-first/first grade multiage classroom.

Students are carefully selected based on their developmental needs. Only children whose parents agree to this placement are put in this setting. These students have the option of staying with the class for one or two years based on teacher observation and parental support. This arrangement allows some students additional learning time in a continuous progress configuration without being in a separate extra-year classroom.

Schools should not eliminate the self-contained pre-first program until the pre-first/first multiage classroom is well under way.

Q. How does multiage education work in a year-round school?

A. Multiage and year-round education are two very compatible concepts. They both focus on continuous learning, developmental readiness, and the elimination of outmoded concepts such as the conventional calendar and grade levels.

Implementing only year-round education supports the belief that learning occurs all twelve months of the year, yet forces students to move lockstep from grade to grade. Implementing multiage education into a school without a year-round calendar allows students to grow developmentally, but only between the months of September and June.

It is important to consider that, since the implementation of the multiage program requires greater effort and time by the staff, a year-round calendar needs to provide regular breaks throughout the year for the staff to rejuvenate.

For information on year-round schools, contact the Executive Director at:

National Association for Year-Round Education (NAYRE)
P.O. Box 711386
San Diego, CA 92171-1386

Q.

Isn't the multiage reform just reinventing the "little red one-room schoolhouse"?

A. Yes and no. The multiage concept combines the best of both worlds.

The one-room schoolhouse provided a community atmosphere where students worked and learned together, as they did in their families and neighborhoods. Students grouped in the one-room schoolhouse learned from each other and had role models available on a regular basis.

Teachers report that children in a multiage setting are less competitive, more cooperative, and as a result are more caring. If one talks to a teacher or student who has experienced the one-room schoolhouse, one can't help but notice the warmth the memories evoke. Current multiage classrooms bring the sense of community of that era back into education.

There are obvious differences between the "little red schoolhouse" and our present form of multiage continuous progress education. Today's world is much more complex and puts very different demands on students than in the era of the one-room schoolhouse. On the other hand, modern students have many more resources, technological and otherwise. Students are placed in a more sophisticated and innovative educational system than the children of the past.

Barbara Nye, Executive Director of the Center for Basic Skills, believes that the multiage organizational structure and instructional climate reflect basic assumptions about how children learn, and utilize teaching practices that maximize the benefits of interaction and cooperation among children. Multiage education takes children where they are and encourages them to grow as far as their minds and abilities can take them.

Multiage education typically builds learning units into themes so all students can ascertain new knowledge on the individual's own learning level. At the same time, each student can observe other students of different levels and acquire additional skills.

For teachers in a multiage classroom, the work is demanding and strenuous, but most agree it is well worth the effort. When educators see children learning, cooperating with each other and caring for each other, they may be right to feel that the future will be better because we are borrowing the best ideas from our past.

A. The term timebound refers to learning which is rigidly controlled by the clock and calendar. In most graded schools, time is the constant, and learning is meted out in 180 five-and-a-quarter hour days per year for thirteen years. Interestingly, the model for this fixed-in-time, graded school system came from Prussia about 150 years ago when efficiency was the goal of industry.

The underlying (and erroneous) assumption behind this model is that all children learn at the same rate. Many children simply need more time to learn, and without it they never manage to reach high performance standards.

There is a well-founded fear among today's educators that American students will not attain world class standards. According to the report of the National Commission on Time and Learning, *Prisoners of Time,*

> In our current timebound system, this fear is well-founded. Applied inflexibly, high standards could cause great mischief.
>
> But today's practices — different standards for different students and promotion by age and grade according to the calendar — are a hoax, cruel deceptions of both students and society. Time, the missing element in the school reform debate, is also the overlooked solution to the standards problem. Holding all students to the same high standards means that some students will need more time, just as some may require less. Standards are then not a barrier to success but a mark of accomplishment. Used wisely and well, time can be the academic equalizer.

The timebound structure currently in place in our schools is considered to be the major design flaw of the American education system. The multiage classroom is a "time breaking" configuration that can provide the flexible learning time necessary to meet the academic as well as the developmental needs of most students, and can correct that flaw.

Q.

What is meant by the term "timebound structure"?

Q.

What does the research say about nongradedness?

A. The most comprehensive look at research on this topic can be found in *Nongradedness: Helping it to Happen* (Anderson and Pavan, 1992). Anderson and Pavan reviewed 64 research studies published between 1968 and 1990. They found, based on normed, standardized achievement and mental health tests, results generally favored nongradedness.

Specifically regarding achievement:

58% of the studies favored nongraded grouping;

33% showed the same growth in graded and nongraded groupings;

9% showed nongraded groups performed more poorly than graded groupings.

Regarding mental health and positive school attitudes:

52% of the studies favored nongraded groupings;

43% showed graded and nongraded groups to be similar in performance;

5% showed nongraded groups performed more poorly than graded groups.

The following excerpt from the Anderson and Pavan book reveals that:

1. A nongraded environment is particularly beneficial for [African-Americans], boys, underachievers, and students of lower socioeconomic status in terms of their academic achievement and mental health.
2. Longitudinal studies indicated that the longer students are in a nongraded program, the more likely it is that they will have positive school attitudes and better academic achievement.
3. Attendance in a nongraded school may improve the students' chances of good mental health and positive attitudes toward school.

A. During the industrial revolution of the 1840s there was considerable immigration to the United States, as well as large scale urbanization. With this huge population influx, there arose an urgent need for mass public education.

In 1843, while in Prussia, educator Horace Mann observed the practice of classifying and dividing students by chronological age for the purpose of creating instructional groupings called grades. In 1848 the Quincy Grammar School in Boston was founded, based on the Prussian model. Pupils were grouped by grade and were either retained or promoted at year's end. The graded structure blossomed in the large urban areas, but not in the rural areas; there were too few students to economically subdivide by grades. Out of this graded movement came the establishment of teacher training schools, graded textbooks, and legislation which set age of entry and curriculum standards.

Over time, the drawbacks to graded education became evident. The assumption that students of the same chronological age were all developmentally equal, socially, emotionally, physically and cognitively, possessed the same learning styles, and required the same time for learning has been found to be false.

Q.

Where did the graded school structure come from?

Q.

What would the student population in a well-balanced multiage classroom look like?

A. As with other classrooms, the individual characteristics and needs of the students should be considered when creating the class. Include an equal number of students from each grade level, and mix the population for gender, age, race, learning abilities and interests. Children with special learning needs should also be included; however, too many special needs students create an imbalance that makes it harder for the teacher to provide good instruction to all of the students in the room.

A classroom with a good balance of students will allow the teacher to group children appropriately for instruction; and children will be able to form friendships and working relationships that foster emotional and social development.

A good rule is to always have the classroom's composition reflect the population of the greater school community.

Q.

What is the physical layout of a multiage classroom?

A. The layout of the classroom should offer whole group gathering areas, table areas for paperwork, areas to relax and share in, and quiet, secluded spots for small instructional groups or impromptu student-led lessons. Ellen Thompson, a primary multiage teacher in Colchester, Vermont, describes her classroom.

My classroom is about 800 square feet; this year it holds 24 children.

The hub of the classroom is a small, rug-covered News area. I give children directions and hold special events here. I also have four large table areas, plus two sets of cubbies which contain over thirty storage spaces for the kids and me.

Also in the room, separated by the cubbies, are two couches. These are used as a quiet sharing spot for all children. There are also two computer centers. These tend to be active and noisy.

My children have places to talk and explore. All materials are at their fingertips, and tables are arranged to encourage discourse.

The classroom is organized by the children, who take care of it throughout the school year. I feel that their ownership of the space and the rules for taking care of it is of the utmost importance.

The physical layout of Thompson's classroom can be seen in the videotape, "The Nuts and Bolts of Multiage Classrooms."

Q.

Are there potential drawbacks to a multiage classroom?

A. Yes! Every reform has its drawbacks, and multiage classrooms are no exception.

Paying attention to the following potential pitfalls will help assure a smooth transition to a multiage classroom.

• *Neglecting Gifted and Talented Students.* This is a major parental concern. Every effort needs to be made to challenge advanced learners, while making sure these students are not taken advantage of as free teachers' aides to tutor less knowledgeable students.

• *Assigning a Marginal Teacher to a Multiage Classroom.* Students should never be subjected to a poor teacher for one year, let alone two or three. (Fortunately, marginal teachers usually don't offer to teach in such a demanding classroom environment.) The principal can quiet parental fears by ensuring that only the highest energy, most qualified teachers will be assigned to teach in multiage classrooms.

• *Perpetuating a Dysfunctional Class.* It seems every few years a school ends up with a class with an unusually difficult combination of students. It is unfair to everyone involved to keep this group together in a multiple-year placement. This class is overwhelming to teach, and is unfair to the students, parents, and teacher.

• *Concentrating Too Many Problem Students in One Class.* Keeping too many high-impact students together in a multiple year placement is a form of tracking. The effect these students have on each another as well as on the teacher often produces negative results.

• *Placing Too Many Handicapped Students in One Class.* There may be a tendency to overload a multiage classroom with special-needs students due to the accommodating nature of the program. Steps must be taken to assure that the multiage classroom does not turn into a special education room or a dumping ground.

• *Masking a Learning Disability.* When grade lines are deemphasized, it is not unusual for a student with disabilities to be inadvertently overlooked during the first year in a multiage classroom. The oversight may delay much needed special education intervention.

• *Keeping Difficult Parents More Than One Year.* Having unreasonable, difficult parents for even one year can be very trying for the teacher. It is in everyone's interest not to force parents and teachers together against their will.

• *Creating Too Much Diversity Among Students.* Too much is too much! When the range of ages and abilities is too great it becomes nearly impossible to meet the wide variety of needs. This environment becomes unworkable and too stressful for the teacher. Too much student diversity is the reason most often attributed to the failure of a multiage program.

• *Clashing Student/Teacher Personalities.* In rare cases an unresolvable personality clash develops between a teacher and student. Moving the student to another classroom seems to be the best way to extricate the child from this unpleasant situation. Schools would be wise to have a policy in force to handle this dilemma should the occasion arise.

Q.

What are some of the wrong reasons to create a multiage classroom?

A. As with many educational endeavors, educators sometimes find themselves in a position for what they consider the wrong reasons. This can be true for multiage programs.

The reasons, other than philosophical, cited for starting a multiage program often involve funding. Some schools have started multiage programs in order to eliminate a staff person or to equalize the size of classes at different grade levels, others in an attempt to justify a larger class size.

In some districts, multiage education has been thought of as a means of restructuring. Some administrators have supported multiage education so that the district would receive recognition for being on the "cutting edge of reform."

One misguided and potentially harmful reason for starting a program is to place students who haven't experienced much school success into the program with the hope that, somehow, a multiage organization will benefit the children.

While it's best to start a program for philosophical reasons in the belief that the multiage structure is best for children, starting a program for other reasons does not necessarily condemn the program to an early demise.

A. If implemented properly, you will see some benefits right away!

During the first year, expect to see students demonstrating industriousness, independence, and self-reliance. Students report a new-found excitement for learning and discover a love for school.

In the second year of the program, teachers report improved student attendance, an overall higher level of discipline, more altruistic behavior, and enhanced self-concepts. There is also a noticeable increase in parental involvement.

Educators report that well into the third year students perform well academically on standard measures. Students also exhibit confidence as they work with a broad range of classmates of varying ages and abilities.

Q.

How soon should we see positive results in our multiage classrooms?

Q.

Wouldn't it be easier to just individualize instruction rather than create a multiage setting?

A. If the only purpose of schooling were to instruct children at their individual levels of learning and there were only a few students in the classroom, it might make sense to individualize instruction for each student. However, many of the benefits of multiage education would be lost if students worked only as individuals.

The research on nongraded education summarized by Pavan and Anderson (1992) in their book *Nongradedness: Helping It to Happen,* shows that students in nongraded programs usually do as well or better on academic measures as students enrolled in single grade programs. This would suggest that on academic measures, there isn't a large difference between students involved in a nongraded structure and students involved in a single grade classroom.

Many of the benefits of multiage education accrue from placing children of mixed ages together. In their book, *The Case for Mixed-Age Grouping in Early Education,* Katz, Evangelou, and Hartman list several social advantages of children in a mixed age setting:

1. Older children exhibit leadership behavior;
2. Friendships occur between children of different ages;
3. Mixed age groups enhance the responsibility of older children;
4. Children play as freely as in same-age groups;
5. Students' self regulation appears to improve.

Since our objective in school is to educate the whole child, we must look at all aspects of a child's development when considering what structures to employ when we invite children into a school setting. Because mixing ages in a multiage classroom has social benefits, a multiage setting that capitalizes on social benefits *and* academic benefits is preferable to an individualized setting in which students would excel in an academic realm only.

A. For one thing, it never really got going! There were many reasons that this reform stalled.

A lot of different programs were competing for funding and the attention of the education establishment. Unfortunately, these programs came on the heels of the "back to the basics" movement spurred by the launching of Sputnik, which created a backlash against any educational programs considered permissive. There were also simultaneous, conflicting reforms such as departmentalization, time-on-task, mastery learning, grade-specific basal text adoptions, standardized testing, and more.

These reforms made it almost impossible to get the multiage/nongraded concept off the ground. For this reason, many programs were created in name only and were not even close to being nongraded. Because most educators were never fully trained in the philosophy of multiage education, there was a lot of anxiety and frustration.

One principal involved in the nongraded wave of the 60s reflected back on his experience, stating why he felt his school's endeavor never got fully implemented.

> "We never fully understood the magnitude of the change and the commitment that was involved. There was a lack of understanding at all levels that in order to implement nongradedness, the school system would have to give up well-entrenched traditional graded practices.
>
> The community just wasn't ready to let go of a system that had been in place for so many years. The lack of real commitment translated to a low level of funding, which in turn hampered proper training, purchasing of instructional materials, staffing needs, and classroom renovations and furnishings. We were defeated before we started."

Often, multiage programs were implemented for the wrong reasons, such as cost savings. Education reforms based solely on financial considerations rather than a pedagogical basis usually have a short shelf-life.

Q.

Wasn't nongraded education tried in the sixties? Why did it fail?

Other reasons have been cited for the demise of the nongraded movement:

- The lack of understanding of authentic assessment led to poor recordkeeping and reporting practices.
- The kindergarten-through-sixth-grade program was still time-bound, as students were expected to complete their tasks in seven 180-day lockstep school years. There was no real provision for students to progress at their own rates.
- There was a lack of supplemental teaching materials available.
- The continuous progress classroom didn't fit the traditional time schedule.
- Teacher training institutions did not prepare teachers with the instructional strategies required for the multiple-grade classroom. Many teachers felt ill-prepared for the tasks required.
- Parents demanded specific grade-level designations as well as letter grades.

With the deck stacked overwhelmingly against educational change, it's no wonder a reform which radically departed from the conventional wisdom of gradedness was difficult to implement and sustain.

Q.

Why do you think the multiage/ ungraded classroom has been so successful in the 90s?

A. Circumstances are very different now than in the 60s. Educators know a lot more about how children learn than they did three decades ago. Many of the elements crucial to the success of multiage education are in place in some form in most schools. Examples include the adoption of developmentally appropriate practices and whole child instructional strategies, such as authentic assessment, writing process, literature-based reading, thematic instruction, and learning centers. The multiage movement of the 60s was destined to fail, because most of these practices had not been adopted when educators attempted to implement multiage programs.

As important as knowing what works well is knowing what practices are developmentally inappropriate and therefore not in the best interest of the child. (These practices are listed on page 93.) In the past, these practices were obstacles too great to overcome for most educators.

Today, numerous publishers have responded to educational change by producing a wide variety of child-centered supplemental instructional material. They have also produced an abundance of professional "how-to" books on implementing, teaching, managing, and assessing instruction in the multiage classroom.

Overall, research on nongraded education has produced favorable results. This factor alone may explain the widespread support from most education groups.

Most educational reforms over the past two decades have been dismal failures and have drained limited resources. The public is clamoring for meaningful education change that works; multiage education works.

Teachers embrace the multiage classroom because they know having students for more than one year is in everyone's best interest. The 150-year-old concept of collecting children by age and segmenting them by grade is now known to be not in the best interest of the child. The wide developmental range of today's students dictate that we teach children in mixed-age groupings. The multiage classroom makes this possible.

Finally, most schools have moved away from the traditional autocratic form of leadership to shared decision making. The system makes teachers and parents important stakeholders. This important change alone accounts for the success of many multiage classrooms.

Q.

Is there a danger that the multiage classroom will become a "dump and hope" program?

A. Yes. Unfortunately, this can be a danger in any classroom. If the multiage program is started with the belief that any and all children, regardless of the severity of their difficulties, will thrive within the program, then the program may be doomed to failure because of the unrealistic demands placed upon the teacher and students. Every classroom should have a balance of students with varying needs and abilities and there should be many reasons for the success of a particular classroom grouping. Don't overload the multiage classroom with high-maintenance children, or you will turn it into a special education class.

34

Do Students Really Benefit From Multiage Education?

Q.

What are the benefits to students in a multiage classroom?

A. There are a wealth of benefits to a student lucky enough to attend an effective multiage classroom. One major benefit is the continuity it provides the student, who has the opportunity to stay with the same teacher and experience the same routines over a two- or three-year period. And since teachers are already familiar with many of their students from the previous year, they don't have to sacrifice instructional time getting to know a whole new class of students each year.

Academically, students get to see a wider spectrum of learning as they work with other students ahead of them and behind them in the learning process. The subject matter itself can be more integrated in a multigrade setting, resulting in less fragmentation.

Socially, students develop a sense of caring and nurturing as they help each other learn. Where everyone is learning at different rates, there is usually less competition; a multiage setting eliminates "faster, better, smarter." And in a setting where students are by nature supporting and assisting each other, real leadership qualities have a chance to emerge.

The multiage classroom actually provides more realistic social interactions for its students; in real-life, adult situations, no one is grouped by age or ability.

A multiage continuous progress program can accommodate a whole range of learning styles and abilities; students with physical, emotional and cognitive disabilities are more readily integrated into a multiage, whole learning setting than into a traditionally structured single-grade classroom.

Yes. Every effort should be made to build in success when selecting a group of learners for placement in a multiage classroom. This careful planning will help educators avoid criticism from detractors that the multiage classroom is: for at-risk students; a "boys club"; a special education program in disguise; a slow learners' class; or only for children from a low socioeconomic background.

These accusations can be minimized by following these criteria:

- Always seek parent permission for student placement.
- Select an equal number of students from each grade level.
- Select an equal number of boys and girls.
- Select an equal number of ages.
- Reflect the racial/cultural mix of your community.
- Select the same number of mainstreamed students as would be placed in a single grade.
- Represent all ability levels in the selection. Take great care to balance the program with students of lower ability and higher ability. The goal should be a mixture of students in a heterogeneous setting.

A well-balanced student population is an important cornerstone of your program.

 Are there student selection criteria for creating a well-balanced multiage class?

Q.

Is chronological age at school entrance a concern in a multiage primary?

A. Yes, but chronological age may be slightly less of a factor for entrance into a multiage classroom. A good multiage program accounts for a wide variance of student maturity, skill levels, cognition, and learning styles. Thus the differences among pupils are dealt with by teachers as part of the normal diversity within the room.

However, having a multiage classroom does not guarantee that the curriculum has also changed. If the pupils are diverse, but the curriculum remains essentially a lockstep, paper-pencil, sit-still, workbook/ditto, and competition-based program, then the issue of chronological age begins to rear its head again.

Research indicates that boys develop more slowly in most aspects, physically, socially, and emotionally, than do girls. Add to this that the youngest pupils are more likely to experience problems with the traditional school program, and you have a major potential problem for most of the youngest males and some of the youngest females as well. These problems have little to do with race or socioeconomic status.

According to Dr. James Uphoff (1995):

The chronologically younger children in any grade are far more likely than the older children to:

- have failed a grade
- become dropouts
- be referred for testing for special services and special education
- be diagnosed as Learning Disabled
- be sent to the principal's office for discipline problems even when in high school
- be receiving various types of counseling services
- be receiving lower grades than their ability scores would indicate as reasonable
- be behind their grade peers in athletic skill level

- be chosen less frequently for leadership roles by peers or adults
- be in special service programs such as Chapter 1
- be in speech therapy programs
- be slower in social development
- rank lower in their graduating class
- be a suicide victim
- be more of a follower than a leader
- be less attentive in class
- earn lower grades
- score lower on achievement tests

> — *Real Facts from Real Schools: What You're Not Supposed to Know About School Readiness and Transition Programs,* by James K. Uphoff, Ed.D.

Q. Do some multiage classrooms have a student population that is too diverse?

A. Yes! As a matter of fact, too much diversity will undermine the integrity of any classroom. The multiage classroom has a much greater age range and a wider range of developmental levels, as well as a host of ability levels. Add to this classroom the increased number of students with learning disabilities, from dysfunctional families, with health problems, with emotional problems, or from poverty, and the magnitude of the diversity becomes staggering.

Too much diversity is one reason many educators cite for the demise of their multiage program. It is for this reason most schools blend only two grades rather than three, and when possible most students are carefully selected for placement in a multiage classroom. See page 37 for information on the criteria for student selection.

Q.

Why do students
seem happier
in a multiage
classroom?

A. They're happier because they're successful in school. They are continuously moving ahead and being recognized for their successes on a daily basis.

Multiage education emphasizes building upon strengths — which builds self-esteem. It also focuses on the whole child, not just his academic skills; a child's gift for social interaction or artistic expression is valued as well.

Multiage classrooms develop into "family," with emphasis on caring, cooperation, and collaboration. Children are at once learner and teacher, the older and more advanced children guiding and providing models for younger, less advanced learners.

Multiage classrooms adapt to the individual needs, interests, and learning styles of the students. Curriculum is adjusted and instructional strategies and the learning environment modified to accommodate the uniqueness of each learner.

The multiage classroom becomes a positive, nurturing, and safe environment for its students. When this type of environment is provided, the result is happy children.

A. There are fewer discipline problems in multiage classrooms. This doesn't happen, however, in a few days, but over months and years of being in a positive environment.

Discipline problems naturally decrease when students are happy and experiencing success in school. Because some of the basic tenets of a multiage classroom are cooperation and continuous progress, students usually do not compete with their classmates, and all students can feel academically successful. The absence of competition and the focus on cooperation and acceptance of individual differences are why multiage classrooms have fewer discipline problems.

Discipline problems in a multiage setting diminish when students:

- are with the same teacher for more than one year.

- stay together in a school family for more than one year.

- know the classroom routine.

- experience consistency over time.

- are placed with older role models.

- experience a high level of cooperative activities in a mixed-age setting.

Q. Why do students in a multiage classroom seem to have fewer discipline problems?

Q.

What kind of discipline program would be appropriate for a multiage classroom?

 A good discipline program for a multiage classroom is one that reflects the following:

1. Students experience themselves as a community of learners, supporting one another's success in the classroom.
2. Students have opportunities to demonstrate that they are responsible and capable people.
3. Students learn to respect their own and others' humanity in the classroom.
4. Students are treated with respect and dignity even when they are being disruptive.

In this classroom, the teacher may involve students in setting up the discipline program. Students are given opportunities to offer suggestions for the kinds of rules or agreements they will create. There may be a "Responsible Citizen" committee that offers or recommends support systems needed by students who have chronic problems in the classroom. A "pay back" system can be set up where students are made aware of the contribution each of them makes to a successful classroom environment. When an individual has threatened the safety or success of the classroom, she is required to give something back — some action that will contribute to classmates to make up for what she took away.

The teacher reads stories and has discussions about anger, frustration, and fears that children have, both in and out of the classroom. Systems are set up to support students who have problems with these issues. A "cooling off" area can be made available with drawing materials, journals, clay, teddy bears, pillows to punch, toy telephones, puppets, etc.

Some children require more structure and support than others. Some are very distractible and impulsive and require systems that assist them in developing the ability to focus and wait for what they want and need. Others have learned that whining, temper tantrums, or defiance are ways to get what they want. These children need to learn from a supportive and nurturing teacher how to communicate their needs appropriately.

Discipline programs for the multiage classroom must be consistent with the overall philosophy of developmentally appropriate education. Students express themselves differently and require a teacher who is aware and able to accept and work with each child wherever she is in her growing process.

A classroom can offer a safe and nurturing learning environment if behavior issues are thought of as a learning process. The three questions every teacher must ask are:

- What does this child need (i.e., attention, power, motivation)?
- What does this child need to learn (i.e., to communicate, to be responsible)?
- How can I provide what this child needs in a loving and supporting manner?

Discipline programs that support this kind of philosophy are reflected in books such as *Loving Discipline A to Z, Cooperative Discipline, Positive Discipline,* and *Discipline with Dignity* (see bibliography.)

Q.

Do children in a multiage setting have better mental health?

A. Yes; however, no organizational structure in and of itself will give young children better mental health. Children develop good mental health when their mental, physical, emotional, and social needs are met in a nurturing environment.

Research does show that students in nongraded programs have more positive attitudes toward school than students in graded programs, and that students in nongraded programs score higher on affective measures than their counterparts in graded classrooms.

What isn't clear from this general research is exactly what kinds of instructional practices were being used in the classrooms studied. It makes intuitive sense that when a child experiences a school environment in which he feels successful and competent, then he will like that school and make positive judgments about himself.

Starting a multiage program will not necessarily improve the mental health of young people. Providing developmentally appropriate experiences that allow students to grow in a variety of ways is probably the best way for the school to contribute to a child's mental health.

A. No. Children will not automatically catch up in a multiage classroom. This seems to be wishful thinking on the part of some school officials seeking a "quick fix," no-cost solution to the issue of developmental differences. Students who are developmentally younger than their peers when they enter a multiage classroom will exit the same way — developmentally young.

Some educators claim that the multiage classroom is an education equalizer. It is not. Varying amounts of learning time — the often unacknowledged factor that can make a difference in student performance — is the equalizer. Children who are developing more slowly may need the extra learning time afforded by the multiage continuous progress classroom.

In a first/second grade multiage blended classroom, some learners may take up to three years to complete the program.

Q. Will children who are developmentally young catch up in a multiage classroom?

Q.

When some developmentally young children take an extra year in a multiage classroom, is this considered retention?

A. No. Some educators would consider this retention; most do not. Rather than arguing whether a developmentally young child is being retained by spending extra time in a multiage program, a better question might be, "Are this child's needs being best served by spending extra learning time in this program?" If the child's social, emotional, physical, and academic needs are being met and if the child is making progress in all of these areas, the question should be, "Why wouldn't we want to keep the child in this placement?"

If the child's needs are not being met, the parents and educational staff should meet to determine how to improve the child's educational program as well as the setting(s) in which the child's needs can best be met. This might mean moving the child to a different educational setting or modifying the child's academic program in the current setting.

There is no academic failure or stigma associated with remaining for additional learning time beyond the traditional two or three years in a multiage classroom.

Q. What about the older students in a multiage classroom? Do they learn when they teach the younger students?

A. The answer to this question is one of the toughest for many people to accept. The norms we all grew up with in a graded system led us to believe some things about older children. And these beliefs were usually quite right, given the boundaries of the graded system. Older children knew more. Older children were smarter. Older children were bigger. And, older children learned faster than younger children.

It's reasonable to ask of what benefit is a multiage classroom to the older children. Won't their learning be slowed down? Won't they act less mature because of the presence of younger children? Won't they lose valuable instructional time because the teacher will be spending more time with the younger children?

There are no studies dealing specifically with the older child in a multiage setting. However, there is evidence that children in well-constructed, multiage, nongraded settings do progress well enough and some say better than their cohorts in single-aged settings.

Even in graded settings there is often a ceiling effect, an upper limit on content for a given grade imposed by a graded curriculum. There are many children in single-grade classrooms who aren't progressing as well as they could because the teacher has to pace her instruction to stop at a certain point, to avoid overlap with the next grade's curriculum.

In a well-functioning multiage classroom, the children are looked at developmentally. This means they are assessed for where they really are, not for where they should be given the "norms of all third graders." Guess what happens when we look at children this way? Some younger children calculate math better than some older children. And some of those older children read better than some of the younger children. And some don't. Some younger children ask questions that cause older children to look at the problem in new ways, and some of the older children explain a solution to younger children in remarkable ways.

In a graded, teacher-centered classroom, by far the largest

amount of interaction is taken up with teacher talk. In a multiage classroom, much more of the interaction is taken up with student talk. We know from years of research on effective schools that higher rates of engaged, directed, student talk is correlated with achievement gains. The older children have as much to gain from this condition as the younger children.

Grouping children solely by chronological age may aggravate misbehavior because, developmentally, we have children misbehaving in roughly the same way because they are roughly the same age. Spread out the age range in a group and you decrease the sameness of misbehavior at any one age.

If the multiage setting is a good one, it will be a better place for the olders as well as the youngers.

Q.

Will the older, gifted child be adequately challenged in a multiage classroom?

A. Yes. As a matter of fact, a good multiage classroom can be a more challenging environment, with greater opportunities for advanced students. One reason is that the multiage setting has a higher ceiling on the curriculum to reflect the needs of the wide range of abilities. There are also opportunities for the more knowledgeable students to teach others. Students who teach other students often retain as much as 90% of the material taught.

On an interpersonal level, older, more knowledgeable students who may be socially and/or emotionally young have an opportunity to socialize with younger class members.

Multiage students get the chance to be the oldest members of a group every two or three years. (Some students in a single-grade classroom may go through childhood without ever experiencing this.) It is beneficial for students to have experiences in different social strata. Older, more knowledgeable students also have more opportunity to be placed in leadership roles. Being needed and admired by younger, less able students increases a student's self-concept.

The following chart compares the opportunities for advanced students in single-grade and multiage classrooms:

Gifted and Talented Children

Single Age/Grade Classroom	Multiage/Multiyear Classroom
• Extended learning program	• Extended learning program
• Tutoring opportunities offer a "teaching" role	• Tutoring opportunities offer a "teaching" role
	AND
	• There are younger children to socialize with.
	• Students can gain "senior citizen" status.
	• The older, more knowledgeable have the chance to practice being in a leadership role.
	• Multiage classrooms have a higher ceiling on the curriculum.

Q.

How does a multiage classroom facilitate the inclusion of differently-abled students?

A. A multiage classroom contains children of different ages and wide ranges of ability, working together in a cooperative setting. Its members are instructed at their own level, learn at an individual pace, and learn on a continuum. This cooperative, interactive setting facilitates inclusion of the differently-abled. Support personnel for the special needs students provide assistance for all or part of the day.

Students with disabilities show more significant gains when placed in a mixed-age classroom (Bailey, Burchinal, McWilliam 1993). These settings provide multiage behavioral role models, a variety of activities, and hands-on learning. These students also benefit especially well from being with the same teacher for multiple years.

A. There are no hard-and-fast rules about how long a teacher and student should stay together. If the relationship between them is a positive one, there are advantages to continuing the relationship over two, three, or even four years. This lets the teacher start each fall knowing the child's academic, social, and emotional needs. Teachers who have students for more than one year report that they can start the year more productively since they don't have to spend the first few weeks of school getting to know the students.

For families that find school intimidating, there is a sense of security and familiarity in knowing the child's teacher from year to year. Once a positive relationship is established between a child's home and the teacher, it is easy to continue this relationship from year to year.

For many children, school is the longest stop in a day filled with many different adults in many different settings. With single-parent families, or families in which both parents must work to support the family, the children often start the day at a childcare facility before being transported to school. After school, the child might return to a childcare facility before being picked up and going home. For these children, the security of having one adult whom they see on a regular basis is probably very important.

Everything that is positive about keeping a child for more than one year can be negative if the child and the teacher do not get along, or if the teacher is unable to meet the child's academic, social, and emotional needs. If any placement isn't helping a child, there is no reason to continue that placement for several years.

Q.

How long should a child stay with the same teacher?

Q.

What if a teacher is concerned about having a difficult child for more than one year?

A. Without effective intervention techniques for the difficult child, this would be a valid concern. Looked at from another angle, however, it's an opportunity for more time to apply effective interventions and encouragement to make a long-term, positive change in this child's life.

All children need to belong, and to feel connected to their classmates and teacher. Being in the same class for two or three years gives a child a sense of security, continuity, and stability.

Difficult students sometimes have issues of trust. A multiyear placement gives these childen more time to bond with the teacher and build that trust. In return, the teacher can provide consistent acceptance, affection, and discipline in a caring environment, which will help a child feel valued and secure.

If a teacher consistently uses encouragement and applies effective discipline interventions, there's a good chance the difficult student will become cooperative before the first year is over; then the teacher can enjoy a good relationship with the child.

In *Cooperative Discipline*, Linda Albert talks about the three C's of encouragement: helping the child feel capable, connected, and contributing. In a multiage classroom, there are many more opportunities to apply these than in a regular classroom. Older kids helping younger students get all three C's at the same time! Cooperative learning activities and classroom meetings also provide them simultaneously.

Consider the possibility that the difficult child is a child with special needs. This child may or may not qualify for services. What better place can his learning style be honored than in a multiage setting, where kids have a better chance at having individual learning needs met? Many borderline or fall-through-the-cracks students will thrive in this environment.

Some techniques that frequently help a difficult child include individual conferences with the student, involving the child in making decisions that affect him, praise and encouragement, contracts, time-out, and behavioral consequences that are related, reasonable, and respectful.

Using effective teaching practices and discipline interventions, honoring learning styles, and adding heavy doses of encouragement all help win over the difficult child. This, done on a consistent basis over a period of two or three years with the same teacher, has an even stronger chance of succeeding than if the child has a different teacher every year. What a gift for the child!

Q. What are our options for handling a personality clash between a child and her teacher?

A. First, what is meant by a personality clash? Is such a perceived clash caused by who the teacher is, who the student is, or by teacher and student behaviors that consistently lead to conflict? Often behaviors that continually lead to conflict are labeled personality conflicts.

The teacher and student should become involved in a conflict resolution process to establish the issues and try to arrive at a solution which is of mutual benefit to both. If, after sincere effort at problem solving, it is apparent that the problem is going to continue, the school should consider changing the class placement of the student. Neither the child's best interest nor the teacher's is served by continuing a situation in which there is a continuous, unsolvable conflict.

Q.

Are there some children who may not be served well in a multiage classroom?

A. Yes! There may be individual cases where a child's needs are not being met in a multiage classroom. However, the problem tends to be with the system or parent and not the student.

Students will not be served well in classes that have been developed for budgetary reasons rather than for optimal learning. Students will not be served well when their parents are ill-informed regarding multiage.

Multiage classroom teachers must receive adequate training and preparation. Developmentally appropriate practices must be in place to benefit all children.

Q.

Is there any danger of a multiage teacher delaying referring a special needs child?

A. Yes. The organization of the multiage classroom deemphasizes grade-level barriers. Multiage teachers view students as learners in a two- or three-year program that is continuous progress. Without rigid grade barriers it is possible for a teacher to inadvertantly overlook a child with a potential learning disability.

By nature the multiage classroom provides a wide spectrum of learning activities, with effective teaching adaptations in place. Active learning, natural language learning, student choices, manipulatives, and documented progress are part of the multiage class.

Children who normally would be classified as "delayed" or late learners often find a level of comfort in a multiage classroom and may not be referred until all interventions have been tried and teachers are unable to document even the smallest amount of progress.

Q.

What will happen to a student in a multiage classroom should he transfer to a single grade?

A. If a student transfers from a multiage classroom, having experienced successful activities including whole learning experiences, cooperative activities and hands-on learning, to a more traditional classroom with large group instruction, basal readers, and workbooks, he will be an unhappy learner!

However, most young children readily adjust to changes. When they are with their parents, they behave one way, with their grandparents another way, and at a friend's home still another way. They expect things to be different when they go to a new classroom or to a new school, and they behave accordingly.

Even the most traditional teacher feels that it is necessary to nurture individual children, and will, to the best of her abilities, make children feel comfortable and successful within the classroom setting.

What is My Role as a Teacher?

Q.

What are the qualities to look for in a good multiage teacher?

A. A good multiage teacher has most of the same qualities as a good single-grade teacher, except that he sees the benefits of the non-graded organization. A good multiage teacher teaches multiage because he wants to, not because he has to.

Multiage teachers share beliefs about learning that inform their teaching practice. They view children as whole beings. They understand that children's learning is influenced by their emotional side as well as their cognitive side.

Multiage teachers are learners. They constantly adjust their ideas and plans based on what they are learning about how their children are learning. For them, assessment is woven into their teaching practice. They constantly assess their students as they employ a variety of teaching styles to tap the broad range of ability present in their rooms. They teach for deep knowledge, knowledge that comes of integrated, long-term thematic study. They work hard teaching basic skills, but they develop knowledge of the basics in an instructional context that is both motivating and successful for children.

Multiage teachers know the importance of language in the classroom. Their classrooms encourage interactions among people, things, and ideas. They are informal settings, comfortable yet bounded by routine, filled with concrete, hands-on, often overlapping activity where children work with each other and learn from other children's conversations.

Multiage teachers create a community of learners in their classroom. Some use classroom meetings, some use cooperative learning groups, some even create the companionship of time among their children. Whatever it's called, this sense of "family" is taught and encouraged so everyone, as much as is possible, feels safe within the group. When this happens, children feel free to take risks, since error becomes only one more step on the path to a better answer.

Finally, the multiage teacher implements flexible groupings. Good multiage teachers group children for selected kinds of skill teaching; on the basis of common interest; to provide variations in language skills and learning modalities within a group; and, sometimes, to teach to students with a particular learning modality. What they do not do is group children consistently by one or two traits so that a child's status is defined by the group to which she regularly belongs.

For examples of how multiage teachers approach their work, see *Multiage Portraits* (Rathbone, Bingham, Dorta, McClaskey, and O'Keefe 1993).

Q.

What are the advantages to teachers who teach in a multiage classroom?

A. In a multiage classroom the teacher has more time to establish relationships with the children, learn their strengths, and to do in-depth evaluation of each child's progress.

There is less instructional time lost in a multiage classroom, since students who attended the same class in the previous year come into the classroom knowing the routine. The teacher can easily assess what skills and concepts have carried over the summer.

A multiyear placement allows the teacher, student, and parents to establish long-term educational goals; and it gives the teacher the advantage of knowing the family better and understanding the family's and child's needs in relation to the school.

In a multiage setting there is less pressure to "cover everything" in a specific period of time; and, since much of the learning takes place between students rather than being wholly teacher-directed, with peer tutoring a real possibility at times, the teacher is free to give more attention to individual students or small groups when appropriate.

It is valuable to the teacher to be able to view all abilities in one classroom, to observe various stages of child development and learning styles, and to see differences in the ways the children of different levels approach a particular task.

Team teaching is not a requirement for a successful multiage classroom, but it has definite advantages in many respects.

The first year a teacher begins using the multiage model, a team partner can provide emotional support during the critical period of adjustment inherent in any change. Also, each teacher in the team will bring her knowledge of the abilities and developmental milestones of children from a specific grade level. Pooling this knowledge will help the teachers ease into working with the two or three different grade levels that will exist in the new multiage classroom.

In the area of curriculum, team teaching is beneficial as well. When the two teachers plan lessons by collaborating and sharing their experiences and ideas, the resulting curriculum is richer. In their research, Goodlad and Anderson (1987) found that "Teachers are enthusiastic about the opportunity to pool differing talents . . . and then confer their instructional plans." They can capitalize on their strengths and even share teaching responsibilities based on subject matter expertise and/or personal interest. Both teachers could teach science but one could teach biology and the other chemistry.

Team teaching also allows children to interact with more than one adult. This aspect of teaming may be very important in the multiage structure, where children stay with the same teacher for two or three years. Teaming lessens the chance of a major personality conflict as children have the opportunity to work with more than one teaching style. "Teaming [in the multiage classroom] permits long-term relationships of children with teachers while also allowing a variety of adults to be involved." (Goodlad & Anderson 1987).

For student assessment, team teaching allows one member of the team to step back at times and really observe children. With two people "kidwatching," at-risk children are less likely to fall through the cracks. In addition, when conferencing with parents and/or resource specialists, the team can provide input based on the observations of two sets of trained eyes, not just one. Parents are often more accepting of information about their child if it is based on the observations and findings of more than one person.

Q.

Is team teaching a critical component of a multiage classroom?

Anderson and Pavan (1992) note that, "[in a team situation] there is the opportunity for pooling data, impressions, and recommendations, and the result is . . . a much more comprehensive view of a child."

In *Team Organization: Promise — Practices and Possibilities*, authors Thomas Erb and Nancy Doda state,

> On the surface, team organization is deceptively simple. It involves only four basic elements: a common group of students, common planning time, a common block teaching schedule, and a common team area. Yet when teachers take full advantage of these four elements, their work life is fundamentally changed, as is the support system for students. Communications patterns within a school change, teachers' involvement in decision making improves, instruction better serves the needs of students, the curriculum is transformed, and teachers find the practice of their profession more rewarding.

Of course team teaching is not the answer for all multiage teachers. A successful team is dependent on two or more teachers who share the same educational philosophy and discipline style. However, according to Goodlad and Anderson (1987), if two (or more) people are compatible, "the ideal school . . . is one that practices nongrading vertically and team teaching horizontally."

A. Yes, it can be. Whether teaching in a multiage classroom is harder work than teaching in a traditional setting depends largely on the teacher. Successful teaching in a multiage environment requires a teacher with a firm philosophical understanding of child development and continuous progress, who recognizes and appreciates different paces of growth and learning; who respects the uniqueness of each child; and who believes strongly that children benefit from this type of learning experience.

How the teacher perceives his role is crucial. If one's belief is that the child is solely dependent on the teacher to learn, the multiage classroom is a more difficult setting in which to teach. It is imperative in a multiage continuous progress class that the teacher sees himself as a facilitator and co-learner and creates an environment which promotes community and trust. The teacher empowers the students by giving up "control" and recognizing that students learn from each other in both formal and informal ways. When everyone in the class is a teacher and learner, diversity becomes a plus, and the shift in the teacher's role makes his job a lot easier.

Another important factor to consider is how comfortable the teacher is with certain teaching strategies and styles. A teacher whose preference is to stand in front of the class, instructing whole group lessons, will most likely be frustrated in a mixed-age environment.

To meet the diverse needs of all the students, teaching takes on a different look. Active, experiential, process learning is imperative. Children work in large groups, small flexible groups, cooperative groups, and individually. The curriculum is integrated, often around a theme or concept which is meaningful and relevant to the student. Learning centers, projects, and "explore" times are prevalent.

In a continuous progress model, many activities are open-ended, allowing each student to bring to it her own level of ability. This way, children are able to successfully move at their own pace without the teacher preparing a separate curriculum for each child. Without a comfort level and understanding of this

Q.

Isn't teaching in a multiage classroom harder for the teacher?

type of teaching, the teacher may find the multiage classroom a difficult endeavor.

Most importantly, to teach successfully in a multiage classroom, the teacher must be motivated by challenge, and be flexible, believe in the underlying concepts, and care about children! Learning to teach in a different environment is a process which takes time, dedication, and the desire to be in that environment. It might not be for all teachers.

As with students, teachers need permission to take risks, and the opportunity to progress at their own pace. The transition to teaching in a multiage class, while natural for some, does not occur overnight. Yet, with collaboration and continued support, it can be a wonderfully fulfilling journey.

A. Multiage works best in learning-centered schools. These are schools whose faculties believe all children can and should learn. Their mission is to enable all children to experience the reward of tough work and joyful learning. Their responsibility is to follow their mission with a common voice. A faculty who really believes this and works on it despite the challenges that face them every day will experience success in moving to a multiage environment.

Faculty from a teaching-centered school may be very competent and effective teachers. Because their focus is on teaching, however, the failure of children is often seen as inevitable, a fault of the child and the child's parents. In a teaching-centered school, children are not the focal point. Coverage of the curriculum is.

Q. What specific staff development training is vital to teaching in a multiage class?

The move to multiage is not about saying one teacher's style is better than another's. Staff development that focuses on this issue, directly or indirectly, will end up in failure. Many failed staff development efforts result from the balkanization of faculty around this issue.

Teaching-centered schools may wage a battle of styles when someone suggests a shift to multiage organization. Faculty fail to see that teachers, no matter whose style may be at issue, are not the point. Children's learning is the point.

The very first issue that should be asked in a staff development effort is, "what can we, as an entire faculty, do to make this school a better learning environment for all our children?" If this is the question, and if teachers are serious about its pursuit, staff development can be successful. If teachers can't focus on the learning of all children, then they will be hesitant to change routines they've developed over years of teaching to make teaching predictable, efficient, and, ultimately, self-serving.

The commitment of a faculty to the learning of their children can begin in many places. Small steps are recommended. Try several multiage projects over the course of a year before jumping into a full-blown multiage classroom. Study how your project goals have been realized and talk constantly with a partner about how it's going. Any one of the following content areas create clear opportunities for multiage teaching success.

• Learn to work increasingly with heterogeneous groups. Reading the works of Roger and David Johnson, Elizabeth Cohen, Robert Slavin, Jo Anne Reid, and others in the cooperative grouping field can be helpful.

• Learn to teach your thematic, interdisciplinary units more holistically, from the instigation of children's interests. Reading the works of Ruth Gamberg, S. Christopher Stevenson and Judy F. Carr in the thematic teaching field can be helpful.

• Learn to balance your skill-based math teaching with hands-on, heterogeneously-grouped project math and problem solving. Reading books by Char Forsten, Marilyn Burns and David Whitin will help.

• Learn that students are motivated when they feel the potential for success in an activity they value. Read what Jere Brophy has to say about motivational theory.

Any one of these places is a good place to start. Of course there are more. Choose one that's comfortable and remember to dialogue with your colleagues about what's happening. Speak and listen. Extend your practice. Expect of yourself what you expect from your children. That is what good staff development is all about.

Note: The above-referenced authors are listed in the bibliography of this book.

Q.

What happens if a teacher discovers he is not meant to teach in a multiage classroom?

A. Teachers placed in a setting for which they do not have adequate preparation or in a setting which places unattainable expectations on them are bound to conclude that they are not meant for the situation. Teachers should not be asked to teach in a multiage teaching situation without the requisite training and strong administrative support for the assignment.

If, after receiving preparation for the assignment and administrative support for the challenge, a teacher still feels he is not meant to teach in a multiage situation, then he should not be required to teach in such a classroom. It serves no purpose to have an educator teach children in a setting where the educator feels he cannot meet children's emotional, social, and academic needs.

Q.

Should a teacher be assigned to a multiage class against her will?

A. No! Teaching well in a multiage classroom is by far more difficult than a single grade. Therefore, it is critical for the teacher to demonstrate a high level of excitement and commitment to this type of classroom organization.

There is an adage, "A person convinced against her will is still of the same mind." This certainly is true when it comes to pressuring a teacher to accept a multiage classroom assignment.

We must remember that just because a person is an excellent teacher in a single grade classroom does not mean she would automatically be suited to teach in a multiage classroom.

An ideal multiage teacher would:

- be an experienced teacher.
- want to teach in a multiage classroom.
- think about students' developmental levels.
- have experience teaching several different grade levels.
- be a risk taker.
- be open to change.
- be well-versed in whole-child instructional strategies.
- be comfortable challenging the status quo.
- know what doesn't work.
- not be a "consumer of fads."
- value developmental diversity.
- be a high-energy person.
- have common sense.
- like collaborating with fellow teachers.

A. NO! You are being set up for failure. These concepts are inconsistent and incompatible with multiage continuous progress education. Teachers who are asked to operate a multiage classroom using a graded philosophy complain of having a high stress level.

If you are being asked to implement a multiage classroom without changing any existing graded elements . . . Don't do it!

Q.

I am being asked to teach our first multiage classroom, but I can't deviate from graded practices that include standardized testing, comparative reporting, homogeneous grouping, and grade-specific basal adoptions. Should I teach this class?

Q.

Isn't every teacher a multiage teacher?

A. No. Every teacher is a mixed-age teacher. People who purport that every teacher is a multiage teacher are referring to the fact that most classrooms have students of different or mixed ages. This does not make it a multiage classroom.

It is true that most single-grade classes are comprised of students who are of differing ages. A typical first-grade classroom could have children as young as five years of age and as old as seven. Although there is a mix of ages, the philosophy, curriculum, instructional practices, and time with the teacher may not be congruent with a multiage continuous progress classroom.

There are important variables when distinguishing a multiage classroom from a single-grade classroom of mixed ages. First, students of different ages and abilities are intentionally placed in the multiage classroom. The curriculum is designed to be a continuous progress curriculum that allows students to progress academically and socially at their own individual rates. The students are usually placed into the multiage classroom for at least the equivalent of two school years, and in some schools for as long as three school years.

Although students in a single-grade classroom might be of mixed ages, they may not be placed with a teacher for more than one year, and the students undertake to master a single-grade curriculum rather than a continuous progress curriculum.

How Do I Know My Students are Learning Anything?

Q.

How do report cards work in a multiage nongraded classroom?

A. Assessment in the multiage classroom is a key to a successful continuous progress program. The teacher must be aware of the individual child's progress in each of five areas: social, emotional, physical, cognitive, and aesthetic.

Record keeping in the form of observations, anecdotal records, taping, and checklists must all be used to assess progress. Portfolios of children's work can also provide valuable evidence of progress in reporting to parents.

Traditional report cards do not show what a child has accomplished. A developmentally appropriate checklist of the five areas, a structured narrative report that responds to set goals, and quarterly conferences should be used in place of a traditional A-B-C-D-F or S(atisfactory) – U(nsatisfactory) report card.

The books *Full Circle: A New Look at Multiage Education*, by Penelle Chase and Jane Doan, *Together is Better*, by Ann Davies, Colleen Politano, and Kathleen Gregory, and *Primary Thoughts: Implementing Kentucky's Primary Program*, by the Kentucky Department of Education, give examples of reports that assess children's progress using developmentally appropriate standards.

Q.

Is it ever appropriate to group by ability or attainment in a multiage classroom?

A. Yes. Short-term ability or attainment grouping occurs in a multiage classroom for a specific purpose. The groupings in the class are extremely flexible and based on tasks, objectives, and materials available. Students move freely in and out of whole groups, small groups, and independent groups.

When convening small instructional groups, it is sometimes necessary to convene the group based on the student's level of achievement on a specific skill or concept. It is also appropriate to convene small instructional groups by interest, student social needs, and a variety of other criteria.

It is important that these groupings be flexible and not rigidly kept in place after the need that caused the group to be convened no longer exists.

Q.

What is the role of standardized achievement testing in the multiage continuous progress classroom?

A. Standardized achievement tests are neither accurate nor reliable measures of children's learning in primary classrooms. They do not coincide with the way children learn or with the curriculum which underlies the instructional model. Furthermore, norm-referenced standardized tests have many of the following side effects:

• They are racially, culturally, and socially biased (Nebraska Dept. of Education 1993).

• They corrupt the process of teaching and learning, becoming ends in themselves rather than means to assess educational objectives.

• They often result in the inappropriate labeling of children, which can change or limit their educational experiences and opportunities.

• They focus time, energy, and attention on easy-to-test, lower-level skills and away from higher-order thinking, creative endeavors, and originality.

• They are poor predictors of student potential, and they do not promote learning.

• Timed tests cause stress, and the neocortex of the brain shuts down under stress. The best way to get a true measure of what a child knows is in an informal, relaxed environment (Hart 1983).

• Standardized achievement tests give false information to the public regarding the status of learning and teaching in American schools (Kamii 1990).

The following professional organizations have written position statements recommending the elimination of group standardized tests for all young children: the National Association of Elementary School Principals, The National School Boards Association, the National Association for the Education of Young Children, and the Association for Childhood Education International.

There are times, however, when these tests can provide useful information about a specific child. When used by a trained professional as an individual diagnostic tool, the results can be helpful in making recommendations about special needs, support services, and instruction. This type of assessment is only required for a small number of children, and its purpose is completely different from the mandated district-wide administration of standardized achievement tests.

Q.

Our administration wants to implement multiage continuous progress classrooms as a way to increase standardized achievement scores. Will multiage classes raise the scores dramatically?

A. No. The desire for higher standardized test scores is not a good reason to implement a multiage program. Although research into nongraded education, which is an aspect of the multiage structure, showed better test scores than the graded classrooms studied (Anderson and Pavan 1992), this research was a comparison between existing nongraded and graded programs. The research team did not study schools as they shifted from a graded to a nongraded structure to see if test scores increased.

Standardized tests measure only a small aspect of a student's capabilities. Her ability to solve problems and to use her knowledge in context, her sense of social responsibility and self-discipline, and her ability to work cooperatively with others will all have more of an impact throughout her life than an ability to pass a single-focus battery test measuring isolated skills.

The multiage structure teaches the same skills regarded so highly by the creators of standardized tests, but does so in a way that is meaningful to the student, and, what is most important, in an atmosphere that allows the student's social, emotional, and physical development to blossom. Those are the reasons to institute a multiage program.

Q. Do you think we will ever be able to stop using grade-level designations?

A. No, not completely. Parent expectations and state-level requirements make it doubtful public schools will ever move away from using grade-level designations completely. However, several reforms are growing within the educational community that will facilitate the deemphasis of grade levels. These reforms include year-round schooling, authentic assessment of students' knowledge and performance, and the blurring of present grade designations by the use of developmentally appropriate practices.

The year-round school concept (sometimes referred to as the 45-15 schedule) will eventually eliminate the current beginning and end of the school year. Students will be seen as continuously enrolled rather than as students in a particular grade for a specific school year.

A nationwide call for authentic assessment of student learning is causing a movement away from letter grades to actual demonstrations of student knowledge and performance. Many districts and states are looking at alternatives such as portfolios of student work, rated apprenticeships, and juried performances. These types of assessment move instruction away from the basal-per-year system that has supported a grade designation system.

How Do
I Explain
Multiage
Education to
the Parents?

Q.

What should parents know about multiage education?

A. As a general principle, parents should not have their young children taking part in any experience they don't fully understand and support. Many parents went through school in a graded structure and consequently see the world through a "graded lens."

Before their child is placed into a non-graded multiage program, parents or guardians should understand several things about the program. First, they should understand the goals for the program and what educators hope to accomplish with the multiage structure. They should also understand what their child's day will be like and what instructional strategies will be used to assist children in their learning.

When talking to parents about the multiage program, it is important to open the lines of communication so that parents know they may approach educators whenever a question or concern arises.

There are several excellent resources that discuss communicating with parents. *Involving Parents: A Handbook for Participation in Schools*, by P. Lyons, A. Robbins, and A. Smith, and *Getting Involved: Workshops for Parents*, by Ellen Frede, are among the books published by the High/Scope Foundation in Ypsilanti, Michigan, which deal with parent-teacher communication. *The Parent Project*, by James Vopat, explains a step-by-step approach to setting up workshops for parents.

A. Parents whose child is in a multi-age program have an opportunity to establish a strong relationship with the child's teacher over a period of several years. This helps the teacher and parents in establishing long-term goals for the child. Parents are also apt to receive more information about their child's learning, since the teacher's evaluation takes place over a longer period of time.

Parents' anxiety levels surrounding a new school year are likely to decrease, since children in the second or third year of a multiage class are already familiar with their teacher, the other children, and the routines of that class. Parents of special needs students in particular can benefit greatly by the presence of a teacher with in-depth knowledge of their child's special abilities and requirements, who can advocate for their child in the decision-making process.

Q.

What are the advantages to parents whose children attend a multiage classroom?

Q.

What are some of the best ways to inform parents about multiage practices?

A. There are many ways, each particular to an individual school community. The best way is to fully involve parent leaders and others interested in restructuring efforts around multiage, nongraded programs.

Before a school makes a decision to move away from traditional methods of school organization, parents must be involved in the decision-making process. Invite them to be a part of school study groups, and have them go on visits to multiage classrooms with school personnel as you research multiage and continuous progress programs. Show parents that your interest and excitement is built on research and conscious study and reflection. Make them a part of that process.

Once the program has started, make sure that parents hear about it on a regular basis. A column in the PTA newsletter can be successful. Make parents a part of ongoing study groups that continue to research multiage education.

Since information on what's happening in the schools will get back to parents anyway, it makes sense for schools to manage the process to assure that parents will get the information they need.

A. Yes. Parents are an integral part of their children's school life, and should be a part of the placement process.

Imagine placing a young child in a multiage classroom, knowing that the parents would prefer a traditional, teacher-up-front classroom. While the child may adapt, it is almost certain the parents will not. School should be accepted and perceived as safe by those who are most important to the child; if it is not, the child is placed in a confusing situation.

Ellen Thompson, a multiage teacher in Colchester, Vermont, describes the placement process in her school:

> I ask incoming parents to meet with their children's kindergarten teacher from the previous year, who gives much of the input for the child's transition. Our school also has a visitation week, where parents are encouraged to come and observe the classroom. We then ask them to write a description of their child and the learning environment they feel will best suit her. The administration uses this information from the parents and the previous teachers in placing the child. Parents are aware that the information they've provided is valued and encouraged. They also are aware that information from teachers and administrators about their child's classroom work and social habits will also be used.
>
> I want the parents of my new students to be very informed about my teaching style, about the complexity of a three-year multiage program, and about the structure and routine of the class. Much time is spent with prospective parents as to the commitment needed from them in a multiage program.
>
> Because my classroom is made up of the children of informed parents, I don't have to spend time defending what I'm doing, even though it may look different than the classrooms the parents attended as children. My students' parents have made a distinct choice for the multiage classroom and are aware of its attributes and its differences from more traditional, single-grade classrooms.

Q. Should parents be given a choice between having their child in a multiage classroom and a single-grade classroom?

Q.

What happens if a child's parents become disenchanted with the multiage classroom?

A. Before a child is placed in any school setting, the parents should be aware of the philosophy of the program and the kinds of experiences in which the child will be involved. There should be on-going communication between the school and family.

If, with this communication, the parents are still disenchanted with the multiage classroom, the school community must work with them to discover the reasons for the disenchantment. Is there a strong philosophical disagreement between the school and the parents? Are there personality differences with the teachers or administrators that make the parents feel alienated from the school? Does their disappointment spring from how a specific academic issue is being addressed?

Once the reason for the disenchantment is uncovered, the usual procedures of problem-solving and conflict management should be employed. Solutions range from clearing up a misunderstanding to changing the child's placement from the multiage program.

A. The multiage classroom organization is foreign to parents who have only experienced the single-grade concept. Often parents report that the traditional, graded classroom worked for them; why should it be changed?

Many parents don't readily recognize the elements of the multiage classroom — whole language, learning centers, theme-based instruction — as analogous to the structured English, math, science, and spelling curriculum they experienced as children.

Multiage practices may bring back memories of the "open concept" of the 60s. Some parents have a legitimate fear based on their own experiences of that structure. Parents need to be reassured that their child will have the best classroom experience possible in a multiage classroom.

Q.

Why do some parents resist the change to the concept of multiage classrooms?

Q.

What about the teacher who has to have the same difficult parents for more than one year?

A. Dealing with difficult or resistant parents can be frustrating and challenging. However, difficult parents are often discouraged parents.

Interacting with parents over two or three years gives the teacher a wonderful opportunity to encourage parents with chances of long term change. In addition, parents and teachers working together enhance student achievement.

If, after explaining the purposes and advantages of multiage practices to parents, there is resistance or apathy, a teacher can do a number of things to foster parental support.

• Send a letter home or make a phone call welcoming the family to the new year and explaining your classroom structure and code of conduct. Invite any suggestions or input parents have on these guidelines. They are important stakeholders in education and should be involved as much as possible.

• Tell the parents about the units or themes you will be covering during the year. Include a list of materials you need for these units that they may have around the house and be willing to donate. This will help parents feel involved in helping the lessons succeed.

• Invite them to visit the classroom. This will alleviate misconceptions parents may have about multiage practices and help them feel that your classroom and school are parent-friendly.

• Send home periodic notes commenting on their child's work. Include stories of the student's positive interactions with children of different ages and show how the interaction affects the child socially and academically. (A number of focus groups in Florida found that hard-to-reach parents indicated they wanted to hear the positive things about their children, not just the negative.) It is essential to share even minimal successes with a child's parents.

• Invite the parents in for conferences and ask how everyone as a team can help the child. This is another effective way to win over a difficult parent. Consider including the guidance counselor or other school personnel if the parents have a history of being very negative or argumentative.

• Recognize that it is impossible to please every parent every day. However, continuing to encourage and communicate with difficult parents will positively affect their relationship with the school and the child.

How
Do We
Implement
Multiage
Education?

Q.

How do we change from single-grade to multiage education?

A. There are different ways to change to a multiage structure, but educators beginning a multiage classroom must be aware of certain aspects of the change process.

Most educators start multiage programs because of a desire to improve the educational experiences they are offering to children. They often visit other programs and classrooms, read professional literature, and have discussions with other educators and parents who are part of the community. From these discussions emerges a philosophy about how a multiage program could best be structured in that particular community. The rationale for the new program is refined and shared with parents, community members, and other educators.

Current resources are inventoried and reconsidered in light of the new program. How will the hands-on math fit the needs of the children in the program? Are there a sufficient number of books available for a class library? What training has been offered to staff in the area of cooperative learning? These resources are applied to the new program structure.

How children will be selected for the program is also part of the change process. Some districts explore parental choice, while in other districts, educators make recommendations regarding which children might benefit from the multiage experience.

A timeline for the implementation of the new program and the continued growth of the program should be developed. An evaluation plan should also be an integral part of implementation.

A. Start by creating a study team with members representing the central office, principal, teachers, parents, specialists, and members of the school board. At your initial meeting, begin by crafting a broad shared vision of your program goals and establish a realistic implementation timeline. This time frame should be a minimum of one year. Study team tasks should include, but are not limited to:

Q.

What are the first steps in starting a multiage program?

• establishing sufficient funding. There will be some expense incurred such as phone, travel, photocopying, an ERIC search, books, etc.

• studying the literature. Purchase multiple copies of a variety of books on the subjects of nongradedness and multiage and multigrade education. (See the bibliography for a complete, up-to-date listing of books and videos. Read the literature; conduct an ERIC search for the best articles.) Read, study, and discuss your findings with your team members.

• working with the support organizations listed in the resource section of this book.

• bringing in an outside expert to assist in orienting and guiding the team. Open this information session to all interested staff.

• attending as many workshops and conferences as possible to be informed of the varying dimensions of multiple-grade practices. Understanding the rationale and theory of multiage education is critical before you proceed any further. You must believe it to see it! When your team is fully committed to the multiage concept, then take the next step:

• visiting multiage classrooms. Investigate a variety of models. Ask hard questions of everyone involved at the schools. Videotape the classrooms if the staff you are visiting will allow you. Talking with teachers who are actually experienced in multiage teaching is the best resource.

• planning the multiage classroom. The team should have gathered enough information to create a comprehensive plan. The following areas should be addressed in this plan:

- **Staff Selection**. Assigning the right staff to the multiage class-room is the key to lasting success. Assign only those staff members who want to teach in a multiage classroom. The ideal staff would have: at least three or four years of teaching experience; an in-depth knowledge of whole language strategies; an understanding of developmentally appropriate practices; an understanding of the change process; and the willingness to be a risk taker.
- **Model Design**. Decide on a classroom model that is workable and acceptable to all involved. A good place to start is either with looping or a two-grade blend. Start small at first. If and when you are ready, add another grade level.
- **Program Budget**. School restructuring is not free! Changing to a multiage configuration will require funding. An adequate budget should include, but not be limited to: supplemental teaching materials; furniture; outside consultants; staff development training; national conferences; school visitations; subscriptions; and organization dues. Adequate financial support is crucial to the success of your program.
- **Staff Development Training**. Teachers assigned to a multiage classroom will find training necessary in the following areas:
  - Cooperative learning
  - Conflict resolution
  - Change process
  - Literature-based reading
  - Team teaching
  - Writing process
  - Learning centers
  - Theme teaching
  - Learning/reading styles
  - Work stations
  - Authentic assessment
  - Manipulative math
  - Hands-on science/social studies

- **Implementation Date**. Set a realistic implementation date. If, when you reach the date, you don't feel ready to implement your program, reschedule. Remember, give yourselves at least a year to plan your program. Don't start until you are comfortable and you feel the elements are in place.
- **Parent Education**. Make parents part of the reconstruction process early on. Multiage classrooms are the most dramatic departure from traditional structure in almost 150 years. The well-being of your program will depend on strong parent support.

Q.

What practices are recommended to make the multiage classroom an effective and efficient organization?

A. First, schools should begin by eliminating or deemphasizing developmentally inappropriate graded practices such as tracking by ability, unfair competition, comparative reporting, grade-level failure, group standardized testing, and social promotion. Removing these graded barriers will open the way for the adoption of more child-centered instructional practices.

Secondly, adopt only classroom practices that are age-appropriate for each child. When you are considering adopting a strategy or practice you might ask yourself several test questions:

- Does this practice address the needs of children or adults?
- Will this strategy become a "solution that contributes to the problem"?
- Is the practice ageless and gradeless?
- Does the practice attempt to control or promote learning?
- Does the practice try to control the amount of learning time available?
- Does the practice discriminate against any group of students?

The answers to these six test questions will help you decide whether a practice helps or hinders the effectiveness of multiage education.

Q.

What obstacles most often impede changing to a multiage classroom?

 Here are a dozen things that will complicate the change to multi-age education:

1. Insufficient planning
2. Starting for the wrong reasons
3. Forcing staff into the program
4. Lack of knowledge about change and the change process
5. Divisions among faculty members
6. Poor class composition
7. Poor communication with parents
8. Poor communication with community members
9. Curriculum that is mismatched to multiage education
10. Insufficient pre-service skills
11. Insufficient in-service and administrative support
12. Inappropriate evaluation and assessment strategies

Any one of these obstacles will impede the implementation of multiage education. One task of the multiage study team is to find ways to work around or eliminate the obstacles.

A. The Concerns-Based Adoption Model, developed by Gene Hall and Susan Loucks at the University of Texas at Austin, is based on the premise that whenever teachers undertake a change, they have concerns about that change.

The first concern is awareness. Educators want to know, "What is a multiage program? What does it look like in action?"

After getting a basic awareness, teachers want more information about the innovation. Visiting schools that have implemented multiage programs can be an excellent way to find out what resources other educators have found valuable. It is also a good opportunity to work through the next stage of concern — personal. Speaking with colleagues who have actually implemented the multiage structure helps to bring the abstract concept of "multiage" into the reality of a group of students in a classroom. Visiting other schools makes it easier to see that multiage programs can be structured and managed in different ways.

Q.

How important is it to visit schools with multiage classrooms before implementing one of your own?

It is possible to implement a multiage program without visiting others, but the tasks of implementing a new program can be made much easier by examining the steps that fellow educators have already taken. It can also help avoid the possible pitfalls of implementation.

Visiting other schools can help create a network of educators interested in multiage practices, who can share resources and expertise and help improve every educator's multiage program.

Q.

What is considered a reasonable time-line for fully implementing a multiage classroom?

 Five years is reasonable in order to develop a multiage classroom in its entirety.

The first year should be taken up by research and development. Year two should include literature-based reading for individuals, with heavy concentration on writing in journals, response logs, etc.

In year three, individualized math should be added, with a concentration on moving from concrete to symbolic to abstract thinking. By year four the curriculum should be finalized and an authentic assessment for parent reporting put in place.

Finally, in year five, the staff should add new, integrated units based on concepts, emphasizing individual projects holistically assessed by the teacher, the individual student, and the student's peers.

Multiage classrooms need to be developed correctly over time. Hurrying the process only sets the teacher up for failure and frustration.

A. Educators wishing to start a multi-age program often wonder about how the program should be configured. Should the program take students from kindergarten, first, and second grade? Should kindergarten be included? How about students who would be assigned to grades 2 and 3?

Successful multiage programs come in a variety of configurations. In some very rural areas, dedicated and knowledgeable educators are creating wonderful learning environments with students ranging from kindergarten to eighth grade. In other schools, educators are starting with a span of two grades.

Q. Is there any one best multiage configuration?

When starting a program, the focus should be on what is *doable* at that particular school, given the school community and the talents of the teaching staff. It is much easier to start with a smaller range of student ages, say three years, and have it be successful than start with too wide an age range and have the teacher overwhelmed and the parents dissatisfied.

When configuring the program, educators have four variables with which to work: age, curriculum, time, and teaching staff. Careful consideration should be given to each variable to create the best possible program for the students.

• Age: Although an age range three to four years is often a good place to start, the individual personalities and developmental levels of the students involved must be considered in addition to the age of the students.

• Curriculum: The curriculum for the class should be built on a continuous progress model. A multiage program cannot be successful if the curriculum for the program must be delivered in a rigid, lockstep fashion.

• Time: Multiage programs have the advantage of having students for more than on year. Some successful multiage programs keep students for two years; other programs are structured to keep the students for three years.

• Staffing: Some teachers teach in a multiage program by themselves; others choose to work with colleagues. While it is certainly possible to implement a multiage program by yourself, working with others in a team teaching situation or a networking group can provide a very valuable support network.

Q.

Is it challenging for a principal to administer a school with both single-grade and multiage classrooms?

A. Yes, it can be challenging. The principal must actively participate in the development of a clearly written set of guiding principles, a philosophy. Researching and writing a school philosophy must involve a consensus of staff, parents, board, central office, and community. The statement should mirror developmentally appropriate principles and practices.

The question of whether single-grade classrooms can coexist with multiage classrooms is easily answered. Yes, they do coexist nicely when both are guided by individually and age-appropriate practices. Implementation of developmentally appropriate practices should precede initiating various grouping configurations.

Indeed, parents desire choices! We must be able to assure parents that whether they choose a single grade, a multiage classroom, multigrade classroom, multiyear classroom, or a team-taught multiage continuous progress classroom that each will be child-centered and developmentally appropriate. What principals must strive for is one philosophy allowing for many configurations.

Q.

How many grades should we blend when we first get started?

A. As the diversity of the student population in a classroom increases, the teacher's workload increases. This holds true for multiage classrooms as well as classrooms in schools that use single grades.

Because of this, it is best to start with two grades when beginning a multiage program. Although this increases the diversity in a classroom, it expands the range only by one grade and age level. As teachers become more comfortable with the two blended grades, other grade levels may be added if the teachers, parents, and administrators feel that a wider range of students will increase the effectiveness of the program.

Q.

Should kindergarten be separated or mixed in with first grade?

A. If your school is adopting a multi-age philosophy, it is important to include the kindergarten in some way for a number of reasons:

• If you want your school community to believe in this philosophy, it's best to be consistent; leaving kindergartners out of a multiage experience when they are a part of the multiage building sends a mixed message.

• Often, the kindergarten teachers in elementary buildings have the most experience in creating developmentally appropriate, child-centered classrooms. Their expertise will be invaluable to teachers who are making dramatic changes in their teaching practices and classroom organization. Don't leave them out!

• Five- and six-year-olds will benefit from a mixed-age environment just as much as seven-, eight-, nine-, and ten-year-olds do. If the priority is a superior, mixed-age environment, then kindergartners deserve to be a part of this experience just as much as any other group.

However, there is no one correct way to group the children in a multiage setting. The most important thing is to consider the specific needs of your students and what your district offers for them, and plan accordingly for your situation.

Combining kindergarten with first grade can be done in a variety of ways. If kindergarten is offered as a full-day program in your school district, there is no reason to separate the kindergartners from the older children.

Many programs combine kindergarten, first, and second grades into one unit with success. One option is to include half-day kindergartners with first graders. The younger children come for the morning only, and the teacher is left with a very small group of six- and seven-year-olds in the afternoon. As the kindergartners mature and possibly need a full-day option, it is available to them.

One classroom arrangement that has drawn some negative response is the combination of two half-day kindergarten programs with one first grade. In this situation, half the children, the first graders, are in the classroom all day, while the other half of the class, the kindergartners, are there either in the morning or in the afternoon. Teachers involved in this situation have not been enthusiastic about the mixed-age grouping. This arrangement adds much more assessment responsibility, recordkeeping, and parental contact to a teaching situation that is already very complex.

Teachers exposed to this arrangement felt it was very difficult to form a cohesive classroom community, and that the older children were often overlooked. It seemed a confusing situation to everyone involved, and so it is not a practice that is recommended.

Another option is combining kindergarten, first, and second grades. While this age span might seem too great, many teachers who have tried it have been very positive about it, especially when there was a team teaching situation. The fact that they had such a variation in levels forced them to give up old "total group" habits and plan their lessons for small groups and/or individual children. This actually made the transition to multiage classrooms less difficult, for they were not falling back on their former, more traditional teaching styles, trying to make the children conform to a new "middle of the road" curriculum, teaching a total group lesson to a nonexistent group of "average" children.

Montessori schools in the United States traditionally have their kindergartners in a multiage classroom with three-, four-, and five-year-olds. This grouping, called preprimary, creates a multiage setting for young children in a half-day program. When children are developmentally ready, they are moved to the primary classroom, another three-year grouping. This situation is nice for several reasons, one of which is the consistency of the multiage, family grouping from the very beginning of school. If your school district offers nursery school and half-day kindergarten, you might consider combining these age groups, rather than K-1.

One of the most appreciated aspects of the multiage school is that it offers alternatives. In your planning, you should consider many options, and choose those that are best for your community.

Q.

What are the most common pitfalls encountered when implementing a multiage classroom?

A. There are numerous implementation pitfalls, and many have dire consequences. Most mistakes, but not all, are avoidable through careful planning.

Unfortunately, much of the available literature on the subject does not acknowledge or address many of the pitfalls associated with multiage practices. "Forewarned is forearmed," says an old adage. Think of the following advice as an early warning to alert you to the pitfalls and to help you avoid the bumpy road to multiage education.

• *Changing the Entire School to Multiage Grouping.* This has proven to be a fatal tactic for many well-intentioned administrators. Some parents do not want this type of program for their child. Educators are strongly urged to offer a variety of placement options. Remember, the attitude, "One shoe size fits all," certainly does not apply to the multiage classroom.

• *Not Considering Parents.* Changing to a multiage classroom is the most significant departure from the traditional graded school structure in almost 150 years. This dramatic change from conventional wisdom is often disconcerting to parents when they don't understand the rationale for it. Parents must be part of the decision-making team. Make parents your partners and you will be well on your way to a successful program.

• *Adopting Too Many Conflicting Mandates.* Most schools today are weighed down with many inflexible rules, regulations, and mandates. Mandates that are all age/grade specific, i.e., textbooks, testing, time-on-task, fixed time policy, make changing to a continuous progress classroom extremely difficult, if not impossible. Request a moratorium on all conflicting mandates. This important incentive will remove the barriers to changing to a multiage classroom.

• *Putting Too Many Grades in One Class.* Some educators stack the deck for success by blending only two grades initially, and end up never adding an additional grade level. The developmental diversity that comes with blending more than two grades often proves too stressful for teachers and can prove to be detrimental to the learners. However, there are many examples of triple-grade blends with team teaching that are very successful.

• *Forcing Teachers to Teach in a Multiage Classroom*. "A person forced against his will is still of the same mind," couldn't be truer in this case. Teachers should never be forced to teach in a multiage classroom against their will. There are many wonderful single-grade teachers who would be inept teaching in a multiage classroom. First and foremost, a teacher must be a strong believer in teaching mixed-ages in a multiple-year placement. It is this deep belief that drives a teacher's dedication and commitment to teach in this type of demanding classroom organization.

• *Creating a Multiage Classroom for the Wrong Reasons*. Often schools are forced to organize multiage classrooms for financial reasons rather than based philosophically on "what's best for kids." Officials perceive multiage education as a money saver and therefore combine grades to equalize class size and/or eliminate a teacher to accommodate an increased student enrollment.

Some educators reportedly have plunged into multiage practices to be the first on their block to be involved in an innovative education reform. Programs organized for the wrong reasons will serve only to build staff resentment and frustrate those that have to teach in these classes. Multiage classrooms that are created for the wrong reasons usually do not have longevity.

• *Not Providing Adequate Staff Development*. Teaching in a multiage classroom requires a great deal of in-service training. Staff development opportunities should include: cooperative learning; whole language strategies; understanding of developmental education; knowledge of the history and rationale for nongradedness; theme teaching; authentic assessment and reporting; ages and stages; literature based reading; process writing; and learning centers. Teachers assigned to teach in a multiage classroom without proper training report a high level of frustration and anxiety. Appropriate training is the teacher's safeguard against program failure.

• *Overstating the Benefits of Multiage Practices*. Multiage grouping is one of the most common-sense reforms over the past 150 years and therefore generates immense enthusiasm and hope. This excitement has been known to propel teachers to overstate the program benefits and virtues. Some think of multiage as some kind of newfound elixir that promises to cure all that ails elementary education. Multiage grouping is certainly not a magic bullet.

Although this type of structure has many wonderful benefits, it is far from a cure-all. Multiage practices are one small, but important element of school reform.

• *High-Speed Implementation.* Once again, educators fall victim to enthusiasm. Our quest for meaningful change often gets us into trouble. Change takes time; lots of it. We strongly recommend one or two years of study and preparation before launching a restructuring effort as revolutionary as multiage practices.

Time is change's best ally. It takes time to study the concept, train the staff, educate the parents, plan the program, and set up the physical environment. The success of your multiage program will hinge on how well you have planned each detail of your program.

• *Creating a Dumping Ground.* The multiage classroom has proven to be one of the most accommodating settings for the inclusion of differently-abled learners. The wide range of abilities, ages, and physical sizes makes differences the norm. Because this diversity forgives differences, there seems to be a temptation to place a disproportionate number of handicapped students in the multiage classroom. Understaffed classrooms become overloaded with special needs students, and quickly become unteachable. Also, parents will rightfully express concern that their child is placed in a "special education" room.

• *Failing to Provide Leadership.* No major restructuring is possible without strong leadership. It is leadership that crafts the shared vision, garners support from the board, parents and fellow staff, and seeks appropriate funding, and other necessary resources.

The principal is the school's cheerleader. She is responsible for the growth and improvement of the entire school program. If the new multiage program is a "school within a school," the principal must delicately balance the care and nurturing of a new mulitage program and the continued support for existing school programs. Care must be taken not to create a "favored son" status for the new program. The principal must distribute accolades and resources on an equitable basis among the school programs.

When the chief proponent for a multiage program leaves the district and support for the program isn't sufficiently established, the new program can be at risk. Leaders initiating new programs should work to build a broad base of support for the new program.

Teachers who are in schools without effective leadership must first establish a strong support system. If support is not forthcoming, don't go it alone. Bringing about educational change is too complex to do by yourself!

A. Teachers should have in place a teaching style which embraces children's individual differences before initiating a multiage instructional setting. The use of open-ended activities and materials lends itself to groups of children working in a variety of ways. These instructional practices help children to accept each other while learning that there is more than one way to solve a problem. Children learn to work with other children of different ages and abilities.

Lucy Calkins talks of the use of grand experiences early in the year which help to bind a group together. Don't wait until June to do that fun field trip, she warns in her book, *Living Between the Lines* (1990). The hike in the woods or the trip to the pond early in the school year really helps to set the tone for the year. The children view each other as whole people with many attributes. They learn to help one another and cooperate with each other as they embark on a special outing. The learning potential is doubled as children learn to move socially as well as academically.

Q. Can you suggest several beginning points where I can try out continuous progress practices without much risk?

Schools can experiment with multiage practices; for instance, a school can ask a teacher to teach a school-wide theme of her choice to children other than her own. This setup helps break down the barriers between teachers as they begin to see that kids are kids. In one such theme study, a school actually worked in multiage groupings as the preferred teaching method. Children were given a list of class choices — anything from candlemaking to beekeeping — and made their choices by content. Teachers were then given groups of students based on the students' topic choices, not their age or ability. The teachers worked with their groups for four days, the groups coming together as a whole school on the fifth day to share newly learned information. Parents, administration, and support staff participated along with teachers and students.

Highly positive, no-fail weeks such as these can do much to create support in a school for a multiage philosophy.

Q.

How do specialists get scheduled in a multiage classroom?

A. All too often, the teachers of art, music, and physical education are not involved in the decision-making and planning processes for starting multiage programs. This can result in a regular classroom curriculum which is ungraded while the curricula for art, music, and physical education are still graded. The specialist teacher must then attempt to teach graded curricula to several different grades at the same time.

The best way to incorporate art, music, and physical education is to involve the specialist teachers from the very beginning of the process. The philosophy of multiage is that students develop at different rates and should be allowed to make academic continuous progress.

These same children presumedly also grow at different rates as musicians and artists, and in their ability to use their bodies. Scheduling the specialists would be less problematic if the teachers in these subjects were teaching curricula which were not rigidly graded.

One way to schedule art, music, and physical education in the multiage classroom is to integrate these subjects into the regular curriculum. This might mean the regular classroom teacher would be responsible for teaching these subjects, or that the specialists would work closely with the classroom teacher to integrate the special areas into the regular classroom experience.

Currently there are few excellent examples of multiage curricula for art, music, and physical education. Several different school systems are working on developing exemplary curricula in these areas and these should be available soon.

Involving specialists in the decision-making process in starting a multiage program, and having solid examples of multiage curricula for art, music, and physical education will make it easier to schedule these subjects in the multiage classroom.

Q. What about special education teachers? How do they fit into a multiage classroom?

A. The multiage class is one of the most inclusive programs a child can experience. The elements and practices are ageless and gradeless, and invitational in nature. These developmentally appropriate, whole-child strategies accommodate rather than discriminate against differently-abled students.

The multiage classroom looks different to students. There is a greater age range, variation of physical sizes, range of developmental levels, and a full span of abilities than in a single-grade classroom. Students placed in a multiage classroom immediately sense that differences are not only normal, but accepted. Also, handicapped students benefit greatly from being assigned to a significant adult for multiple years.

This environment allows special education personnel to work in the classroom most of the time with special needs students, rather than pulling them out for their services. These students get to stay with their supportive peers, while the non-handicapped kids get an opportunity to develop more understanding and empathy for the children who need special assistance.

Classroom teachers benefit from having special education personnel in the classroom as well; the specialists can either become involved in team teaching with the regular teacher, or can act as support personnel and free the teacher for other things.

Some students' needs are severe enough to warrant their being pulled out of the classroom into a resource room for special instruction or therapy, but they return to the multiage environment afterwards, and generally spend much of the day with their classmates.

In contrast, the single-grade classroom is not only age- and grade-specific, but timebound as well. Often this reason alone makes it difficult to mainstream some handicapped students into this type of narrow classroom configuration.

Teachers are quick to agree that the mixed-age, multiyear organization is more conducive to accommodating students with special needs.

Q.

Will a basal program work in a multiage classroom?

A. The multiage teacher looks for instructional practices which complement authentic tasks with authentic materials. That is, the teacher wants her children to read from the same type of books that they might (and do) read at home. Since the multiage curriculum is often dovetailed with the needs and inspirations of the children, most multiage teachers would not be able to (or want to) rigidly follow the regimen offered by a basal company that does not know the needs of those specific children.

Children learn to read best when given choices of reading material along with appropriate practice situations. The use of open-ended activities which allow children to write and spell developmentally are key to multiage programs.

A basal system can be used in such a manner. It should not be used to grade-group or ability-track children within a multiage classroom. Certainly, the teacher should be viewed as the decision-maker as to how these types of reading materials best match her instructional practices.

Q. Help! Two of us want to teach in a multiage classroom, but our principal doesn't like change. He provides no leadership and only wants to maintain what we have.

A. Usually people are resistant to change because they don't understand it or because they've been burned by change in the past. Here's some advice on how to deal with the problem.

First, you should discuss your desire to move toward some of the more developmentally appropriate practices, including whole language, manipulative math, transitional spelling, process writing, and thematic units. If your principal is not familiar with these practices, you could ask for some inservice training for yourselves or the full staff. Be sure to share your information and enthusiasm with other staff members at every opportunity. If you are given the chance to move toward these more developmentally appropriate practices, you are halfway there.

You may need to consider moving toward multiage classes by asking for the chance to begin a looping class with one of your colleagues. (A looping class is one in which the teacher stays with the same group of students for more than one year. One teacher goes on with her class and the other teacher loops back to pick up a new group.) Looping is seen as a less radical change than moving directly into multiage classes. (See page four for information on looping.)

Secondly, if your principal gives you the opportunity to try teaching in a multiage classroom, build it to win! Invite the children of supportive parents to join the class (you can worry about the other parents once the multiage classroom is successfully implemented). Be sure that your colleagues are open to the idea (especially the physical education, music and art teachers), and document your successes at every opportunity. Positive documentation is essential for future support from decision makers who may have been discouraged by past change efforts.

Q.

What should
my principal see
going on in
my multiage
classroom?

A. Upon entry she should observe a sense of excitement and joy within a community classroom environment. Here are some common threads that weave a multiage classroom into a learning tapestry:

• A clearly written, belief statement detailing how children learn and how they shall be taught.

• Teaching practices that mirror developmentally appropriate practices.

• Heterogeneous groupings — class meetings, large groups, small groups, and individuals.

• A variety of ad hoc groupings:
  • interest groups
  • learning styles groups
  • problem-solving groups
  • skills needs groups
  • skill reinforcement groups
  • cooperative groups

• Peers helping peers. Robert Slavin (1989) suggests that students are often more effective at teaching each other than are teachers teaching students. Students helping each other reinforce their understanding of knowledge, skills and attitudes.

• Authentic assessment and progress reports. Teachers should employ authentic observations of each student's process for learning. The teacher relies on student work samples, journals, learning logs, miscue analysis, videos, teacher/student conferences, anecdotal observations, and sociograms as tools for assessment.

• Parents encouraged to attend family conferences. They receive frequent anecdotal reports from teachers. Parents are informed through weekly classroom newsletters of how they may participate in their child's learning week to week.

Q.

Our school is very traditional and we are not allowed to teach using developmentally appropriate practices. Should we implement a multiage classroom?

A. No. You must teach developmentally. Developmentally appropriate practices are at the heart of multiage classrooms. If you must remain with traditional practices, you will find it impossible to teach a multiage classroom.

In traditional classrooms, cooperative learning and student interaction are often missing. These practices are vital to multiage classrooms to show improvement in social development and academic growth. If you can't be developmentally appropriate, do not try to institute multiage education unless it is a means to push for developmentally appropriate practices.

Q.

What steps can we take to minimize staff dissension when implementing a multiage classroom?

A. Some dissension is inevitable when implementing any innovative program. Professional envy, petty jealousy, or hurt feelings do happen no matter how hard we try to avoid them.

There are specific situations we need to be aware of that create divisiveness among the staff. The best preventive measure is good communication.

By being aware of what issues upset fellow teachers, you can take the necessary measures to avoid future problems.

• To ensure success, the administration often places only gifted students in the multiage classroom. This practice causes an ability imbalance with other classes and creates a homogeneous program that tends to be elitist.

• Be careful not to refurbish only the multiage classroom. Fresh paint, new furniture, carpet, and shades can cause petty jealousy.

• Keep the class size in a multiage classroom comparable to single-grade classrooms. Nothing produces staff resentment like unequal class size.

• The multiage classroom should accommodate the same number of special needs students as a single grade. Multiage classrooms should never be exempt from the responsibility of educating handicapped students. Preferential treatment will turn the entire staff against the multiage program.

• Wonderful things are happening in all of the classes in your school, not just in the multiage classroom. Be sure to praise all classrooms when addressing the school board, parents groups, and the media. This alleviates hurt feelings.

• When visitors come to your school, be sure they visit all classrooms, not just the multiage classroom.

• Select the name of your program very carefully. A name such as the Wonder Program, the Platinum Years, or the Shooting Stars could give an air of elitism to your program.

You can take simple steps to avoid difficult situations and bring harmony to the entire staff.

Outside the School Walls: How Does the "Real World" Affect Multiage Education?

Q.

What is the role of the superintendent?

A. In terms of the development and implementation of a multiage program, the role of the superintendent is paramount.

It is the superintendent's responsibility to provide the governing board with all the necessary information (research, rationale, etc.) about the effects of a multiage approach to teaching and learning. This will allow the board to make an informed decision to adopt the program. The board must have a clear and complete understanding of the pros and cons in order to fully support the program.

The superintendent is the spokesperson to the community for the program. The superintendent must always be "out front" supporting the program's implementation. He must find ways to involve the community in this new educational process which affects their children, and must be willing to be the one to deal with critics who would assail the new program.

The superintendent also must provide the multiage staff with an environment free of the fear of failure. The staff needs assurance that the superintendent will provide support and, if necessary, defend them and the program.

A. In many states, the role of the school board or school committee is dictated by state law. Usually the school board creates the policies that either encourage or discourage a multiage structure.

Whenever possible, it's helpful to include board members on the study committee that investigates the multiage concept. They should be part of the decision-making process that determines whether or not a district implements a multiage structure.

It is important for board members to understand the reasons for the multiage structure and the goals for adopting it. They should be updated periodically about the progress of the program.

School board members should be sent copies of any communication with parents; it's usually a good idea to invite them to parent meetings held for parents of children in the program.

School board members have chosen the difficult task of overseeing a school system and charting the educational course they feel is best for the children. The more information they have about program goals and information about how and why children are instructed in the programs, the better able they will be to make quality decisions about programming.

Q. What role should the school board play?

Q.

How can I be sure that multiage continuous progress practices are not just another educational fad?

A. It's fairly easy to tell by asking some straightforward questions. Fads are often associated with meeting the needs of politicians, bureaucrats, and those who have a financial interest at stake. Determining this may be as simple as seeking the right questions, such as whose needs are being addressed.

Passing fads in education have the following elements in common:

- Top-down initiative
- Teacher-centered concept
- Unfunded state mandates
- Designed to meet the needs of "educators" who don't work with children
- Founded on the needs of textbook and test publishers or other special interest groups

Lasting education reforms, on the other hand, generally have these characteristics:

- Bottom-up initiative
- Student-centered concept
- Local site-based decision
- Designed to meet the needs of *all* students
- Founded on the principles of how students learn best

Multiage education reflects how students grow, develop and learn. It's a concept that enjoys the broad support of administrators, teachers, and parents. Multiage grouping is one of the few concepts that has the distinction of having educational research confirm common sense.

A. Some groups oppose almost any new idea in education for several reasons:

Q.

Why do some pressure groups oppose multiage practices?

• We live in a society that is in constant change. Life is not stable; people are struggling with broken families, single parent households, latchkey children, the economy, crime, drugs, technology, and so on. People rely on schools to be the one place that should be steady, predictable and the same as it was when they attended. For that reason alone people may resist any type of change in our schools.

• Since the "Nation at Risk" study in 1984, public education has been evaluated, criticized, and tampered with by every parent, expert, and opposition group. The new fads that we have experimented with in the last several decades have also been scrutinized. While educators continue their search for what works best with students, pressure groups resist the idea of their children being part of an educational experiment. Thus, opposition is on the rise.

• Some pressure groups oppose multiage practices because educators miss the opportunity to effectively communicate with their constituents. At times parents are kept in the dark and only find out about change after the fact. Thus the opposition groups are basing their opinions on half-facts, rumors, and horror stories.

Parents need to be brought into the process earlier, not after the fact. When interest groups feel they have ownership, change will occur more rapidly, and there will be less opposition.

A very helpful book from the Association for Supervision and Curriculum Development (ASCD), *How to Deal with Community Criticism of School Change*, by Marjorie Ledell and Arleen Arnsparger, gives advice in how to deal with pressure groups.

Q.

Is it a good idea to mandate a reform such as multiage practices?

A. Not necessarily. Mandating targets teachers for change, rather than making them agents for change. Recent studies of change show that you can't mandate what matters, and that for change to occur, there needs to be administrative support from above and grassroots support from below. Mandating the multiage structure will not ensure the success of a multiage program.

However, support from the state education department or the central office are important components for the success of any program. If a state department believes the multiage structure to be a viable one, it is less likely to initiate other mandates, such as a graded curriculum, that make it more difficult to implement a multiage structure.

While mandating multiage education doesn't guarantee successful implementation, a strong initiative combined with local knowledge and support can be components of a successful multiage program.

Q.

What is meant by "conflicting educational reform"?

A. Many schools have multiple initiatives in the form of mandates and innovative programs, often adopted simultaneously. Unfortunately many of these initiatives are wholly incompatible with developmentally appropriate practices, the foundation of the multiage classroom. Conflicting reforms tend to distract educators from the real issue and compete for financial resources, and may often be implemented for the wrong reasons.

This dichotomy creates conflict. Examples of reform practices thought to be at cross-purposes with implementing multiage practices include: time-on-task, mastery learning, basal adaptations, standardized testing, comparative reporting, social promotion, and departmentalization. These practices actually create barriers to change. Educators often give up as these obstacles to reform seem too difficult to overcome.

Teachers report a high level of stress and frustration when asked to implement a multiage classroom while being required to adhere to rigid graded practices.

In order to get around this problem, schools nationwide have successfully sought and secured waivers at the local and state levels and bypassed these conflicting educational mandates.

Q.

What are the driving forces behind changing to multiage practices?

A. Since the graded structure came into existence in the Quincy Grammar School in 1848, some people have been critical of it. Today, as in the past, critics feel that schools should be focused on the needs of children. They are concerned that the graded structure forces too many children to be something they are not. Children are forced to read books too difficult for them because reading the book is the expectation for that "grade level."

Having defined grade levels based on a normal curve means that some students must be "below grade level." Critics of the graded structure are concerned about what the label of being below grade level does to students' self-esteem and motivation.

Today there is renewed interest in the multiage organizational structure, because of many educators' desire to be student-centered. The movement has been bolstered by recent advances in understanding of how we teach literacy, mathematics, social studies, and other subject matter. Recent findings about how young children learn, grow, and construct their own meanings have added to the foundations supplied by Piaget, Vigotsky, Gesell, and Dewey. Curricula which allow children to experience content in a meaningful way help them to learn new information.

Where Can I Get More Information on Multiage Education?

Q.

Can you recommend any books on multiage practices that would be good for parents?

A. One good book is *The Nongraded Primary: Making Schools Fit Children*, published by the American Association of School Administrators. This is a good, quick overview, and helpful in introducing the subject.

Two other straightforward, easy-to-read books are *A Common Sense Guide to Multiage Practices*, by Jim Grant and Bob Johnson, and *Multiage Portraits: Teaching and Learning in Mixed-age Classrooms*, by Charles Rathbone, Anne Bingham, Peggy Dorta, Molly McClaskey, and Justine O'Keefe.

A lot of other books that have been published for educators are also suitable for interested parents. Many of these are listed in the bibliography at the back of this book.

A. One of the best places to start looking for information on developmentally appropriate practices (DAP) is the National Association for the Education of Young Children (NAEYC).

Their book, *Developmentally Appropriate Practices in Early Childhood Programs Serving Children from Birth to Age 8* (Sue Bredekamp, ed.) is a wonderful resource for multiage primary teachers.

The main text of the book is devoted to outlining and explaining what is developmentally appropriate for different ages, and what is not appropriate.

This is *not* a book about multiage classrooms. Although NAEYC has published a short book about multiage education, it does not support the continuous progress philosophy of extra learning time if it adds an additional year to a child's education.

Q.

Where can I find information on developmentally appropriate practices?

The National Association of Elementary School Principals (NAESP) publishes a book called *Early Childhood Education and the Elementary School Principal: Standards for Quality Programs for Young Children*. This book tells how to apply developmentally appropriate practices to a school curriculum, and deals with accountability, parents, and community issues.

Developmental Education in the 1990's, by Jim Grant, provides straightforward answers to 92 questions commonly asked about developmentally appropriate practices.

Growing and Learning in the Heartland is a joint effort by Nebraska and Iowa. Its pages are full of concrete and definite ways to shape a developmentally appropriate multiage program. This book is highly recommended for its thoroughness, authenticity, and accessibility.

Constructing Curriculum for the Primary Grades, by Diane Dodge, Judy Jablon, and Toni Bickart, shows how to create a curriculum centered on the developmental stages of children's growth.

Kentucky's State Department of Education's book entitled *Primary Thoughts: Implementing Kentucky's Primary Program* has a very good chapter on developmentally appropriate practices. Chapter six includes a straightforward definition of developmentally appropriate practices as well as strategies to build a DAP multiage curriculum.

Q.

Is there a national meeting on multiage continuous progress practices?

A. There is currently only one national meeting which focuses exclusively on the issues of multiage classrooms. The National Multiage Conference is held each summer, usually at the end of July. This conference is sponsored by The Society For Developmental Education. SDE also offers seminars and workshops around the country on multiage practices. To find out about SDE's conferences and seminars, contact:

The Society For Developmental Education
Ten Sharon Road
PO Box 577
Peterborough, NH 03458
Phone: 1-800-462-1478
FAX: 1-800-337-9929

A. Since 1989 the number of colleges and professional organizations which offer courses and training in multiage education have increased.

The International Reading Association (IRA), American Association of School Administrators (AASA), and the National Association of Elementary School Principals (NAESP) offer multiage workshops at their larger regional and national conferences, as do the Association for Supervision and Curriculum Development (ASCD) and Phi Delta Kappa (PDK).

Many regional education centers such as BOCES in New York and the state principals associations offer regional worshops which include multiage education as one of their topics.

The Society For Developmental Education offers many seminars and workshops across the country on multiage education and other child-centered practices.

Q.

Where can I find training in multiage practices?

Q.

Where can I find support for my multiage program?

A. One of the first and best places to begin looking for support for your multiage program is in your own state. Your state department of education should be able to tell you about other multiage schools in your area.

There are also regional and national organizations that can help support your efforts:

The International Registry of Nongraded Schools (IRONS) is a group created by highly regarded multiage researcher Robert H. Anderson.

IRONS was established primarily to gather information about nongraded schools from the beginning stages through complete implementation. IRONS is used primarily to increase communication in the nongraded community and facilitate research.

IRONS is based at the University of South Florida.

The Multiage Classroom Exchange is sponsored by *Teaching K-8,* the professional magazine for teachers. Teachers send in their names and in exchange receive a list of teachers with which they can correspond and swap ideas and tips.

The National Alliance of Multiage Educators was created as a teacher-helping-teacher network. Established in 1993 and sponsored by The Society For Developmental Education, N.A.M.E. serves as a link between educators from across the country who are interested in multiage education. Membership is open to any educator interested in multiage practices. You do not have to be currently teaching or working in a multiage setting to apply.

The biggest benefit of this network is the ability to find teachers across the country who can answer multiage questions with hands-on experience and knowledge. N.A.M.E. also provides bibliographies to members and distributes a newsletter.

See the resource section of this book for addresses and phone numbers of these organizations.

 Do I have permission to copy the Multiage Bill of Rights?

 Yes, with appropriate credit included.

The Multiage Education Bill of Rights
by Jim Grant

1. Every student has the right to learn in a continuous progress program.
2. Every student should have the option to continue with a teacher for more than one year.
3. Every student has the right to experience continuous success in the academic, social, physical, and emotional areas.
4. Every student has the right to take the time she or he needs to learn in a multiage classroom without the stigma of school failure.
5. Every student has the right to be free from the harmful effects of long-term ability grouping.
6. Every student has the right to learn in a program appropriate for his or her level of development.
7. Every student has the right to learn in a mixed-age classroom with a variety of learners.
8. Every student has the right to learn in a classroom where literacy is taught in an integrated manner.
9. Every student has the right to learn in a classroom where cooperation and conflict resolution are fostered.
10. Every student has the right to be evaluated in a manner that is consistent with how he or she was taught and measures knowledge, skills and attitudes which are meaningful.

Q.

Have we
answered all of
your questions?

A. No. Multiage practices are evolving and growing. If you have a question about multiage practices that we haven't answered, please send it to:

Multiage Q & A
Crystal Springs Books
Ten Sharon Road
PO Box 500
Peterborough NH 03458
FAX: 1-800-337-9929

We will respond to your questions.

RESOURCES

Multiage Organizations

National Alliance of Multiage Educators (N.A.M.E.)
Ten Sharon Road, Box 577
Peterborough, NH 03458
1-800-924-9621

N.A.M.E. is a networking organization for educators who want to share ideas, information, and experiences with others who have a similar interest in multiage and continuous progress practices. N.A.M.E. is also a source of information on books and audiovisual materials about multiage. Membership is open to those considering multiage as well as those already teaching and supervising it.

International Registry of Nongraded Schools (IRONS)
Robert H. Anderson, Co-director (with Barbara N. Pavan)
PO Box 271669
Tampa, FL 33688-1699
813-963-3899

IRONS is housed at the University of South Florida. It has been established to gather information about individual schools or school districts that are either in the early stages of developing a nongraded program or well along in their efforts. Its purpose is to facilitate intercommunication and research efforts. There is a phase one membership and a full membership.

Multiage Classroom Exchange
Teaching K-8
40 Richards Ave.
Norwalk, CT 06854

The Multiage Classroom Exchange puts teachers in contact with others who are interested in swapping ideas, activities, and experiences relating to the multiage, progressive classroom.

To join, send your name, address, age levels you teach, years of experience with multiage education, and a self-addressed, stamped envelope to the address listed. You'll receive a complete, up-to-date list of teachers who are interested in exchanging information.

California Alliance for Elementary Education
Charlotte Keuscher, Program Consultant
California Department of Education
721 Capitol Mall, 3rd Floor
Sacramento, CA 95814
email: ckeusche@smtp.cde.ca.gov

The Elementary Education Office and the California Alliance for Elementary Education have published the second and third installments of The Multiage Learning Source Book.

The second installment is a guide for teachers, principals, parents, and community members who are involved and interested in multiage learning. It contains descriptions of what multiage learning is and is not, questions staffs and parents need to explore before and during the implementation stage, samples of how schools have communicated to their communities about multiage learning, classroom curriculum vignettes, anecdotes from schools that have successfully implemented multiage learning under a variety of conditions, descriptions of multiage programs throughout the state, and current and relevant research and articles.

The third installment deals with evaluation of a multiage program and assessment in multiage classrooms. Copies of the Source Book are distributed free of charge to California Alliance for Elementary Education members.

California Multiage Learning Task Force
(see California Alliance for Elementary Education)

Much of the multiage learning effort in California is guided by the Multiage Learning Task Force, which is made up of California Alliance for Elementary Education teachers, principals, parents, board of education members and university professors. The group has provided guidance and material for The Multiage Learning Source Book and are practitioners of multiage learning.

Networks supporting multiage education are being developed throughout California, coordinated by the Elementary Education Office, which assists the startup of the groups. Once started the groups operate independently.

Newsletter

MAGnet Newsletter
805 W. Pennsylvania
Urbana, IL 61801-4897
email: ericeece@ux1.cso.uiuc.edu

The MAGnet Newsletter provides information about schools that have implemented multiage practices.

ERIC

ERIC (Educational Resources Information Center) is a clearinghouse or central agency responsible for the collection, classification, and distribution of written information related to education. If you need help finding the best way to use ERIC, call ACCESS ERIC toll-free at 1-800-LET-ERIC. If you need specific information about multiage education, call Norma Howard at 1-800-822-9229.

A Value Search: Multiage or Nongraded Education is available for $7.50 and can be ordered from Publication Sales, ERIC Clearinghouse on Educational Management, 5207 University of Oregon, Eugene, OR 97403-5207. A handling charge of $3.00 is added to all billed orders.

Workshops and Conferences

The Society For Developmental Education
Ten Sharon Road, Box 577
Peterborough, NH 03458
Phone: 1-800-462-1478
FAX: 1-800-337-9929

The Society For Developmental Education presents one- and two-day workshops as well as regional conferences throughout the year and around the country for elementary educators on multiage, inclusion education, multiple intelligences, character education, discipline, whole language, authentic assessment, looping, readiness, math, science, social studies, developmentally appropriate practices, special education, and other related topics.

SDE also offers customized inservice training to schools on the topics of their choice.

SDE sponsors an International Multiage Conference each July. For information on workshop/conference dates and locations, or to arrange for inservice training, write or phone SDE at the address or phone/FAX numbers listed above.

BIBLIOGRAPHY

American Association of School Administrators. *The Nongraded Primary: Making Schools Fit Children*. Arlington, VA, 1992. A good quick overview, helpful in introducing the subject. 28 pages.

Anderson, Robert H., and Pavan, Barbara Nelson. *Nongradedness: Helping It to Happen*. Lancaster, PA: Technomic Press, 1992. Carefully establishes a strong theoretical basis for successful nongradedness. Particular attention given to identifying practices that make nongradedness effective. 240 pages.

Banks, Janet Caudill. *Creating the Multi-age Classroom*. Edmonds, WA: CATS Publications, 1993, 1995. 136 pages.

Bingham, Anne A.; Dorta, Peggy; McClasky, Molly; and O'Keefe, Justine. *Exploring the Multiage Classroom*. York, ME: Stenhouse Publishers, 1995.

Bridge, Connie A.; Reitsma, Beverly S.; and Winograd, Peter N. *Primary Thoughts: Implementing Kentucky's Primary Program*. Lexington, KY: Kentucky Department of Education, 1993. Excellent source for specific, helpful advice for teachers starting a multiage program. 254 pages.

Chase, Penelle, and Doan, Jane. *Full Circle: A New Look at Multiage Education*. Portsmouth, NH: Heinemann, 1994. 184 pages.

Davies, Anne; Politano, Colleen; and Gregory, Kathleen. *Together is Better*. Winnipeg, Canada: Peguis Publishers, 1993. 77 pages.

Fogarty, Robin, ed. *The Multiage Classroom: A Collection*. Palantine, IL: Skylight Publishing, 1993. 230 pages.

Gaustad, Joan. "Making the Transition From Graded to Nongraded Primary Education." *Oregon School Study Council Bulletin*, 35(8), 1992. 42 pages.

———."Nongraded Education: Mixed-Age, Integrated and Developmentally Appropriate Education for Primary Children." *Oregon School Study Council Bulletin*, 35(7), 1992. 38 pages.

———."Nongraded Education: Overcoming Obstacles to Implementing the Multiage Classroom." 38(3,4) *Oregon School Study Council Bulletin*, 1994. 84 pages.

Gayfer, Margaret, ed. *The Multi-grade Classroom: Myth and Reality*. Toronto: Canadian Education Association, 1991. Realistic look at problems that can plague combined-grade classrooms. 57 pages.

Goodlad, John I., and Anderson, Robert H. *The Nongraded Elementary School.* New York: Teachers College Press, 1987. A new first section in this seminal book adds a current perspective on the enduring importance of nongradedness. 248 pages.

Grant, Jim, and Johnson, Bob. *A Common Sense Guide to Multiage Practices.* Columbus, OH: Teachers' Publishing Group, 1995. 128 pages.

Grant, Jim; Johnson, Bob; and Richardson, Irv. *Our Best Advice: The Multiage Problem Solving Handbook.* Peterborough, NH: Crystal Springs Books, 1996.

Grant, Jim, and Richardson, Irv, compilers. *Multiage Handbook: A Comprehensive Resource for Multiage Practices.* Peterborough, NH: Crystal Springs Books, 1996.

Gutierrez, Roberto, and Slavin, Robert E. *Achievement Effects of the Nongraded Elementary School: A Retrospective Review.* Baltimore, MD: Center for Research on Effective Schooling for Disadvantaged Students, 1992.

Hanson, Barbara. "Getting to Know You: Multiyear Teaching." *Educational Leadership*, November, 1995.

Hunter, Madeline. *How to Change to a Nongraded School.* Alexandria, VA: Association for Supervision and Curriculum Development, 1992. 74 pages.

Jacoby, Deborah. "Twice the Learning and Twice the Love" (About looping). *Teaching K-8*, March 1994.

Kasten, Wendy, and Clarke, Barbara. *The Multi-age Classroom.* Katonah, NY: Richard Owen, 1993. 84 pages.

Katz, Lilian G.; Evangelou, Demetra; and Hartman, Jeanette Allison. *The Case for Mixed-Age Grouping in Early Education.* Washington, DC: National Association for the Education of Young Children, 1990. A short but careful examination of the benefits of mixed-age grouping. 60 pages.

Kentucky Department of Education. *Kentucky's Primary School: The Wonder Years.* Frankfort, KY. 155 pages.

Kentucky Education Association and Appalachia Educational Laboratory. *Ungraded Primary Programs: Steps Toward Developmentally Appropriate Instruction.* Frankfort, KY: KEA, 1990. Summary case studies of 10 ungraded primary programs with a resource section and samples of strategies used. 100 pages.

Maeda, Bev. *The Multi-Age Classroom.* Cypress, CA: Creative Teaching Press, 1994. 128 pages.

Mazzuchi, Diana, and Brooks, Nancy. "The Gift of Time." *Teaching K-8*, (February 1992): 60-62.

Miller, Bruce A. *Children at the Center: Implementing the Multiage Classroom*. Portland, OR: Northwest Regional Educational Laboratory; 1994. 123 pages.

————.*The Multigrade Classroom: A Resource Handbook for Small, Rural Schools*. Portland, OR: Northwest Regional Educational Laboratory, 1989. This extensive loose-leaf book offers a multitude of examples and suggestions equally valuable to rural, suburban, and urban multiage teachers. 262 pages.

————.*Training Guide for the Multigrade Classroom: A Resource for Small, Rural Schools*. Portland, OR: Northwest Regional Educational Laboratory, 1990. Focuses on preparing teachers.

(Million, June). "To Loop or Not to Loop? This a Question for Many Schools." *NAESP Communicator*, Vol. 18, Number 6. February 1996.

Nye, Barbara. *Multiage Programs: An Interview With Barbara Nye*. Nashville, TN: The Center for Research in Basic Skills, Tennessee State University, 1993.

Ostrow, Jill. *A Room With a Different View: First Through Third Graders Build Community and Create Curriculum*. York, ME: Stenhouse Publishers, 1995.

Politano, Colleen, and Davies, Anne. *Building Connection: Multi-Age and More*. Winnipeg, Canada: Peguis Publishers, 1994. 151 pages.

Province of British Columbia Ministry of Education. *Foundation*. Victoria, British Columbia, 1990.

————.*Primary Program Foundation Document*. Victoria, British Columbia, 1990. This and the accompanying Resource Document provide extensive resources that would be of great help in any multiage program. 362 pages.

————.*Primary Program Resource Document*. Victoria, British Columbia, 1990. 392 pages.

Rathbone, Charles; Bingham, Anne; Dorta, Peggy; McClaskey, Molly; and O'Keefe, Justine. *Multiage Portraits: Teaching and Learning in Mixed-age Classrooms*. Peterborough, NH: Crystal Springs Books, 1993. A penetrating glimpse of how effective multiage classrooms work and how teachers see their role in these classrooms. 185 pages.

Virginia Education Association and Appalachia Educational Laboratory. *Teaching Combined Grade Classes: Real Problems and Promising Practices*. Charleston, WV: AEL, 1990. A realistic look at combining grades. 57 pages.

Audio / Video

Anderson, Robert, and Pavan, Barbara. *The Nongraded School*. Bloomington, IN: Phi Delta Kappa. An interview with the authors of *Nongradedness: Helping It to Happen*. Video, 30 minutes.

Cohen, Dorothy. *Status Treatments for the Classroom*. New York: Teachers College Press, 1994. Video.

George, Yvetta, and Keiter, Joel. *Developing Multiage Classrooms in Primary Grades*. Ft. Lauderdale, FL: Positive Connections, 1993. Video, 22 minutes.

Goodman, Gretchen. *Classroom Strategies for "Gray-Area" Children*. Peterborough, NH: Crystal Springs Books, 1995. Video.

Grant, Jim. *Accommodating Developmentally Different Children in the Multiage Classroom*. Keynote address at the NAESP Annual Convention, 1993. Audiocassette available from Chesapeake Audio/Video Communications, Inc. (6330 Howard Lane, Elkridge, MD 21227, product #180).

————.*The Multiage Continuous Progress Classroom*. Peterborough, NH: Crystal Springs Books, 1993. Keynote address at the 1993 National Multiage Education Conference, audiocassette and video, 52 minutes.

Katz, Lilian. *Multiage Groupings: A Key to Elementary Reform*. Alexandria, VA: Association for Supervision and Curriculum Development, 1993. Audiocassette.

Lolli, Elizabeth J. *Developing a Framework for Nongraded Multiage Education*. Peterborough, NH: Crystal Springs Books, 1995. Video.

Province of British Columbia Ministry of Education. *A Time of Wonder: Children in the Primary Years*. Victoria, British Columbia. Video.

Thompson, Ellen. *The Nuts and Bolts of Multiage Classrooms*. Peterborough NH: Crystal Springs Books, 1994. Video, 1 hour.

————.*How to Teach in a Multiage Classroom*. Peterborough, NH: Crystal Springs Books, 1994. Video, 25 minutes.

Ulrey, Dave, and Ulrey, Jan. *Teaching in a Multiage Classroom*. Peterborough, NH: Crystal Springs Books, 1994. Video.

United Learning. *Mixed-Age Grouping at the Olive-Mary Stitt School*. Niles, IA. Video.

Assessment

Baskwill, Jane, and Whitman, Paulette. *Evaluation: Whole Language, Whole Child*. New York: Scholastic. 1988. 43 pages.

Batzle, Janine. *Portfolio Assessment and Evaluation: Developing and Using Portfolios in the K-6 Classroom*. Cypress, CA: Creative Teaching Press, 1992.

Clemmons, J., Laase, L., Cooper, D., Areglado, N., and Dill, M. *Portfolios in the Classroom: A Teacher's Sourcebook*. New York: Scholastic, Inc., 1993. 120 pages.

Harp, Bill, ed. *Assessment and Evaluation in Whole Language Programs*. Norwood, MA: Christopher Gordon Publishers, 1993. 232 pages.

Kamii, C., ed. *Achievement Testing in the Early Grades: The Games Grownups Play*. Washington, DC: National Association for the Education of Young Children, 1990.

Lambin, D., and Walker, V. "Planning for Classroom Portfolio Assessment." *Arithmetic Teacher*, 41(96), February, 1994.

Lazear, David. *Multiple Intelligence Approaches to Assessment: Solving the Assessment Conundrum*. IRI/Skylight Publishing, Inc., 1994. 205 pages.

Attention Deficit Disorder (ADD) / Attention Deficit Hyperactivity Disorder (ADHD)

Hartmann, Thom. *Attention Deficit Disorder: A Different Perception*. Penn Valley, CA, and Lancaster PA: Underwood-Miller, 1993. 186 pages.

Quinn, Patricia O., M.D., and Stern, Judith M., M.A. *Putting on the Brakes: Young People's Guide to Understanding Attention Deficit Hyperactivity Disorder (ADHD)*. New York: Magination Press, 1991. 64 pages.

Cooperative Learning

Bayer, Ann Shea. *Collaborative-Apprenticeship Learning: Language and Thinking Across the Curriculum, K-12*. Katonah, NY: Richard C. Owen Publishers, Inc.; and Mountain View, CA: Mayfield Publishing Co., 1990. 146 pages. Discusses proximal development theory of L.S. Vygotsky.

Cohen, Dorothy. *Designing Groupwork: Strategies for the Heterogeneous Classroom*. New York: Teachers College Press, 1994.

Curran, Lorna. *Cooperative Learning Lessons for Little Ones: Literature-Based Language Arts and Social Skills*. San Juan Capistrano, CA: Resources for Teachers, Inc., 1992. 153 pages.

Ellis, Susan S., and Whalen, Susan F. *Cooperative Learning: Getting Started*. New York: Scholastic, 1990. 72 pages.

Fisher, Bobbi. *Thinking and Learning Together: Curriculum and Community in a Primary Classroom*. Portsmouth, NH: Heinemann, 1995. 426 pages.

Forte, Imogene, and MacKenzie, Joy. *The Cooperative Learning Guide and Planning Pak for Primary Grades: Thematic Projects and Activities*. Nashville, TN: Incentive Publications, 1992. 142 pages.

Johnson, David, and Johnson, Roger. *Cooperation and Competition: Theory and Research*. Edina, MN: Interaction Book Company, 1989.

————. *Learning Together and Alone*. Englewood Cliffs, NJ: Prentice Hall, Inc., 1991.

Kagan, Spencer. *Cooperative Learning*. San Juan Capistrano, CA: Resources for Teachers, Inc., 1992. 376 pages.

Shaw, Vanston, with Spencer Kagan, Ph.D. *Communitybuilding In the Classroom*. San Juan Capistrano, CA: Kagan Cooperative Learning, 1992.

Slavin, Robert. *Cooperative Learning*. Englewood Cliffs, NJ: Prentice Hall, 1989.

————. *Cooperative Learning*. Boston: Allyn and Bacon, 1995.

Discipline

Albert, Linda. *Cooperative Discipline: How to Manage Your Classroom and Promote Self-Esteem*. Circle Pines, MN: American Guidance Service, 1996.

Curwin, Richard L., and Mendler, Allen N. *Discipline with Dignity*. Alexandria, VA: Association for Supervision and Curriculum Development, 1993. 267 pages.

Glasser, William, M.D. *The Quality School: Managing Students Without Coercion*. New York: HarperPerennial, 1992.

Nelson, Jane, Ed.D. *Positive Discipline*. New York: Ballantine Books, 1987. 243 pages.

Wright, Esther, M.A. *Loving Discipline A to Z*. San Francisco: Teaching From the Heart, 1994. 80 pages.

Inclusion

Goodman, Gretchen. *I Can Learn! Strategies and Activities for Gray-Area Children*. Peterborough, NH: Crystal Springs Books, 1995.

————. *Inclusive Classrooms from A to Z: A Handbook for Educators*. Columbus, OH: Teachers' Publishing Group, 1994.

Bailey, D.B, and Wolery, M. *Teaching Infants and Preschoolers with Handicaps*. Columbus, OH: Merrill, 1984.

Friend, Marilyn, and Cook, Lynne. "The New Mainstreaming." *Instructor Magazine*, (March 1992): 30-35.

Lang, Greg and Berberich, Chris. *All Children are Special: Creating an Inclusive Classroom*. York, ME: Stenhouse Publishers, 1995.

Society For Developmental Education. *Creating Inclusive Classrooms: Education for All Children*. Peterborough, NH: 1994.

Stainback, S., and Stainback, W. *Support Networks for Inclusive Schooling*. Baltimore: Paul H. Brookes, 1990.

Stainback, S., Stainback, W., and Forest, M., eds. *Educating All Students in the Mainstream of Regular Education*. Baltimore: Paul H. Brookes, 1987.

Learning Centers

Cook, Carole. *Math Learning Centers for the Primary Grades*. West Nynack, NY: The Center for Applied Research, 1992.

Ingraham, Phoebe. *Creating and Managing Learning Centers: A Theme-Based Approach*. Peterborough, NH: Crystal Springs Books, 1996.

Poppe, Carol A., and Van Matre, Nancy A. *Language Learning Centers for the Primary Grades*. West Nynack, NY: The Center for Applied Research in Education, 1991. 234 pages.

Wait, Shirleen S. *Reading Learning Centers for the Primary Grades*. West Nynack, NY: The Center for Applied Research, 1992.

Waynant, Louise, and Wilson, Robert M. *Learning Centers: A Guide for Effective Use*. Paoli, PA: Instructo Corp., 1974. 130 pages.

Learning Styles/Multiple Intelligences

Armstrong, Thomas. *In Their Own Way: Discovering and Encouraging Your Child's Personal Learning Style.* New York: Putnam, 1987. 212 pages.

————.*Multiple Intelligences in the Classroom.* Alexandria, VA: Association for Supervision and Curriculum Development, 1994. 198 pages.

Campbell, Bruce. *The Multiple Intelligences Handbook.* Stanwood, WA: Campbell & Associates, 1994.

Campbell, Linda; Campbell, Bruce; and Dickinson, Dee. *Teaching & Learning Through Multiple Intelligences.* Needham Heights, MA: Allyn & Bacon, 1996.

Carbo, Marie. *Reading Styles Inventory Manual.* Roslyn Heights, New York: National Reading Styles Institute, 1991.

Carbo, Marie; Dunn, Rita; and Dunn, Kenneth. *Teaching Students to Read Through Their Individual Learning Styles.* Needham Heights, MA: Allyn & Bacon, 1991.

Lazear, David. *Multiple Intelligence Approaches to Assessment: Solving the Assessment Conundrum.* IRI/Skylight Publishing, Inc., 1994. 205 pages.

————.*Seven Pathways of Learning: Teaching Students and Parents About Multiple Intelligences.* Tucson, AZ: Zephyr Press, 1994. 241 pages.

————.*Seven Ways of Knowing: Teaching for Multiple Intelligences.* Palatine, IL: IRI/Skylight Publishing, Inc., 1991. 254 pages.

————.*Seven Ways of Teaching: The Artistry of Teaching With Multiple Intelligences.* 190 pages.

Vail, Priscilla L. *Learning Styles: Food for Thought and 130 Practical Tips for Teachers K-4.* Rosemont, NJ: Modern Learning Press, 1992. 133 pages.

Other Books and Articles of Interest

Ames, Louise Bates, and Ilg, Frances L. *Your Five-Year-Old, Sunny and Serene.* New York: Dell, 1979. 123 pages.

————.*Your Six-Year-Old, Loving and Defiant.* New York: Dell, 1979. 132 pages.

Ames, Louise Bates, and Haber, Carol Chase. *Your Seven-Year-Old, Life in a Minor Key.* New York: Dell, 1985. 165 pages.

————.*Your Eight-Year-Old, Lively and Outgoing.* New York: Dell, 1989. 147 pages.

————. *Your Nine-Year-Old, Thoughtful and Mysterious*. New York: Dell, 1990. 164 pages.

Atwood, Ron, ed. *Elementary Science Themes: Change Over Time: Patterns, Systems and Interactions, Models and Scales*. Lexington, KY: Institute on Education Reform, University of Kentucky, 1993. Set of four pamphlets, 50 pages each.

Bailey, D.B.; Burchinal, M.R.; and McWilliam, R.A. "Age of Peers and Early Childhood Development." *Child Development* 64: 848-62, 1993.

Banks, Janet Caudill. *Creative Projects for Independent Learners*. Edmonds, WA: CATS Publications, 1995.

Bloom, Benjamin S. *All Our Children Learning: A Primer for Teachers and Other Educators*. New York: McGraw-Hill, 1981.

————, ed. *Developing Talent in Young People*. New York: Ballantine, 1985.

Bredekamp, Sue, ed. *Developmentally Appropriate Practice in Early Childhood Programs Serving Children From Birth Through Age 8*, expanded edition. Washington, DC: National Association for the Education of Young Children, 1987. A position paper that has been influential in primary education. 92 pages.

Burns, Marilyn. *About Teaching Mathematics*. Sausalito, CA: Math Solutions Publications, 1992. 286 pages.

————. *A Collection of Math Lessons: From Grades 3 Through 6*. White Plains: Cuisinaire Company of America, 1987.

Burns, Marilyn, and Tank, B. *A Collection of Math Lessons: From Grades 1 Through 3*. White Plains: Cuisinaire Company of America, 1987.

Calkins, Lucy M. *Living Between the Lines*. Portsmouth, NH: Heinemann, 1990. 315 pages.

Cartwright, Carol A., and Cartwright, Phillip G. *Developing Observation Skills*. New York: McGraw-Hill, 1974. 168 pages.

Davies, Anne; Politano, Colleen; and Cameron, Caren. *Making Themes Work*. Winnipeg, Canada: Peguis Publishers, 1993. 88 pages.

Early Childhood Education and the Elementary School Principal. Alexandria, VA: National Association of Elementary School Principals, 1990. 64 pages.

Eisele, Beverly. *Managing the Whole Language Classroom: A Complete Teaching Resource Guide for K-6 Teachers*. Cypress, CA: Creative Teaching Press, 1991. 139 pages.

Erb, Thomas O., and Doda, Nancy M. *Team Organization: Promise — Practices and Possibilities*. Washington, DC: National Education Association, 1989.

Fisher, Bobbi. *Joyful Learning: A Whole Language Kindergarten*. Portsmouth, NH: Heinemann, 1991. 225 pages.

Forsten, Char. *Teaching Thinking and Problem Solving in Math*. New York: Scholastic Professional Books, 1992.

———.*Using Calculators is Easy!* Scholastic Professional Books, 1992.

Frede, Ellen. *Getting Involved: Workshops for Parents*. Ypsilanti, MI: High/Scope Press, 1984. 306 pages.

Gamberg, Ruth; Kwak, W.; Hutchins, R.; and Altheim, J. *Learning and Loving It: Theme Studies in the Classroom*. Portsmouth, NH: Heinemann, 1988.

Gentry, J. Richard. *My Kid Can't Spell*. Portsmouth, NH: Heinemann, 1996.

Gentry, J. Richard, and Gillet, Jean Wallace. *Teaching Kids to Spell*. Portsmouth, NH: Heinemann, 1993. 136 pages.

George, Paul. *How to Untrack Your School*. Alexandria, VA.: Association for Supervision and Curriculum Development, 1992. Presents the various issues surrounding the practice of tracking. 42 pages.

Glasser, William. *Control Theory: A New Explanation of How We Control Our Lives*. New York: Harper Perennial, 1984.

———.*Control Theory in the Classroom*. New York: Harper Perennial, 1986.

Good, Thomas L., and Brophy, Jere. *Looking in Classrooms*. New York: HarperCollins Publishers, 1991. 605 pages.

Goodman, Yetta M.; Hood, Wendy J.; and Goodman, Kenneth S. *Organizing for Whole Language*. Portsmouth, NH: Heinemann, 1991. 389 pages.

Grant, Jim. *Childhood Should Be A ~~Pressure~~ Precious Time*. (poem anthology) Rosemont, NJ: Modern Learning Press, 1989.

———. *Developmental Education in the 1990's*. Rosemont, NJ: Modern Learning Press, 1991.

———. *"I Hate School!" Some Common Sense Answers for Parents Who Wonder Why, Including the Signs and Signals of the Overplaced Child*. Rosemont, NJ: Programs for Education, 1994.

———.*Jim Grant's Book of Parent Pages*. Rosemont, NJ: Programs for Education, 1988.

———.*Worth Repeating: Giving Children a Second Chance at School Success.* Rosemont, NJ: Modern Learning Press, 1989.

Hall, G.E., and Loucks, S.F. "Program Definition and Adaptation: Implications for Inservice." *Journal of Research and Development in Education* (1981) 14, 2:46-58. These two authors developed the Concerns-Based Adoption Model.

Hart, Leslie. *Human Brain, Human Learning.* New York: Longman Press, 1983.

Heald-Taylor, Gail. *The Administrator's Guide to Whole Language.* Katonah, NY: Richard C. Owen, 1989. 189 pages.

Healy, Jane M. *Endangered Minds: Why Children Don't Think and What We Can Do About It.* New York: Simon and Schuster, 1990. 382 pages.

———.*Your Child's Growing Mind: A Guide to Learning and Brain Development From Birth to Adolescence.* New York: Doubleday, 1987. 363 pages.

Henderson, Anne T.; Marburger, Carl L.; and Ooms, Theodora. *Beyond the Bake Sale: An Educator's Guide to Working with Parents.* Columbia, MD: National Committee for Citizens in Education, 1990.

Herr, Judy, and Libby, Yvonne. *Creative Resources for the Early Childhood Classroom.* Albany, NY: Delmar, 1990. 625 pages.

Johnson, Spencer, and Spencer, Constance. *The One-Minute Teacher: How to Teach Others to Teach Themselves.* New York: Morrow, 1986. 112 pages.

Karnofsky, Florence, and Weiss, Trudy. *How to Prepare Your Child for Kindergarten.* Carthage, IL: Fearon Teacher Aids, 1993. 79 pages.

Katz, Lilian G., and Chard, Sylvia C. *Engaging Children's Minds: The Project Approach.* Norwood, NJ: Ablex Press, 1989.

Kohn, Alfie. *No Contest: The Case Against Competition.* Boston, MA: Houghton Mifflin, 1992.

Kozol, Jonathan. *Savage Inequalities: Children in America's Schools.* New York: Crown, 1991.

Lamb, Beth, and Logsdon, Phyllis. *Positively Kindergarten: A Classroom-proven, Theme-based Developmental Guide for the Kindergarten Teacher.* Rosemont, NJ: Modern Learning Press, 1991. 141 pages.

Ledell, Marjorie and Arnsparger, Arleen. *How to Deal with Community Criticism of School Change*. Alexandria, VA: Association for Supervision and Curriculum Development, 1993. 43 pages.

Lyons, P.; Robbins, A.; and Smith, A. *Involving Parents: A Handbook for Participation in Schools*. Ypsilanti, MI: High/Scope Press, 1984. 248 pages.

Miller, Karen. *Ages and Stages: Developmental Descriptions and Activities Birth Through Eight Years*. Chelsea, MA: Telshare Publishing Co., 1985. 153 pages.

National Commission on Excellence in Education. *Nation at Risk: The Full Account*. USA Research Staff (ed.), 1984. 128 pages.

———.*Nation at Risk: The Full Account*. 2nd ed. USA Research Inc. Staff (ed.), 1992. 128 pages.

National Education Commission on Time and Learning. *Prisoners of Time*. Washington, DC: U.S. Government Printing Office, Superintendent of Documents, 1994.

Nebraska Department of Education and Iowa Department of Education. *The Primary Program: Growing and Learning in the Heartland*. Lincoln, NE, 1993.

New Jersey Education Association. "Class Size: Giving Students a Chance to Succeed." *The NJEA Review* 62 (March 1989): 15-19.

Northeast Foundation for Children. *Notebook for Teachers: Making Changes in the Curriculum*. Greenfield, MA: NFC, 1993.

Oakes, Jeannie. *Keeping Track: How Schools Structure Equality*. New Haven: Yale University Press, 1985.

Pavelka, Patricia. *Making the Connection: Learning Skills Through Literature*. Peterborough, NH: Crystal Springs Books, 1995.

Reid, Jo Anne; Forrestal, P.; and Cook, J. *Small Group Learning in the Classroom*. Portsmouth, NH: Heinemann, 1989.

Routman, Regie. *Transitions: From Literature to Literacy*. Portsmouth, NH: Heinemann, 1988. 352 pages.

———.*Invitations: Changing as Teachers and Learners K-12*. Portsmouth, NH: Heinemann, 1991. 644 pages.

Rowan, Thomas E., and Morrow, Lorna J. *Implementing the K-8 Curriculum and Evaluation Standards: Readings from* The Arithmetic Teacher. Reston, VA: National Council of Teachers of Mathematics, 1993. 105 pages.

Sampson, Michael, ed. *Pursuit of Literacy: Early Reading and Writing*. Dubuque, IA: Kendall/Hunt Publishers, 1986.

Schlosser, Kristin G., and Phillips, Vicki L. *Beginning in Whole Language: A Practical Guide*. New York: Scholastic, 1991. 112 pages.

Sharp, Quality Quinn. *Evaluation in the Literature-Based Classroom: Whole Language Checklists Grades K-6*. New York: Scholastic, 1989. 38 pages.

Stevenson, S. Christopher and Carr, Judy F. *Integrated Studies in the Middle School: Dancing Through Walls*. New York: Teachers College Press, 1993.

Thompson, Gare. *Teaching Through Themes*. New York: Scholastic, 1991. 176 pages.

Uphoff, James K., Ed.D. *Real Facts From Real Schools: What You're Not Supposed To Know About School Readiness and Transition Programs*. Rosemont, NJ: Modern Learning Press, 1990, 1995. 150 pages.

Uphoff, James K. and Gilmore, June E. *Summer Children: Ready (or Not) for School*. Middletown, OH: J&J Publishing Co., 1986. 124 pages.

Vail, Priscilla. *Emotion: The On-Off Switch for Learning*. Rosemont, NJ: Modern Learning Press, 1994.

Vopat, James. *The Parent Project: A Workshop Approach to Parent Involvement*. York, ME: Stenhouse Publishers, 1994. 191 pages.

Vygotsky, Lev. S. *Mind in Society: The Development of Higher Psychological Processes*. Michael Cole et al, eds. Cambridge, MA: Harvard University Press, 1978.

———.*Thought and Language*. Alexey Kozulin, ed. Cambridge, MA: MIT Press, 1986. 256 pages.

Wheelock, Anne. *Crossing the Tracks: How "Untracking" Can Save America's Schools*. New York: New Press, 1992.

Whitin, D.; Mills, H.; and O'Keefe, T. *Living and Learning Mathematics: Stories and Strategies for Supporting Mathematical Literacy*. Portsmouth, NH: Heinemann, 1990.

Wood, Chip. *Yardsticks: Children in the Classroom Ages 4-12*. Greenfield, MA: Northeast Foundation for Children, 1994. 176 pages.

Index